BORN
Again

How to Maximize Your
New Life in Christ.

TO: HONORÉ
ABUNDANT BLESSINGS
IN
YOUR NEW LIFE IN CHRIST!

08.05.19

Jesus answered and said to him, *"Truly, truly, I say to you, unless one is born again he cannot see the kingdom of God."*

John 3:3

BORN AGAIN

HOW TO MAXIMIZE YOUR NEW LIFE IN CHRIST

Ruthven J. Roy

REHOBOTH
PUBLISHING

Born Again: How to Maximize Your New Life in Christ
Copyright © 2012 by Ruthven J. Roy

ISBN: Paperback   978-0-9717853-9-7
                                  0-9717853-9-2

Cover design: Emmerson Cyrille

Unless otherwise indicated, Bible quotations are taken from the *New American Standard Bible,* © 1960, 1962, 1963, 1968, 1971, 1972, 1973, 1975, 1977, by The Lockman Foundation. Used by permission.

Other versions used are
KJV - *The Authorized King James Version,* © 1975 by Thomas Nelson Inc., Publishers.
NRSV - *New Revised Standard Version,* © 1989, by Division of Christian Education of the National Council of the Churches of Christ in the United States of America.
NIV - *New International Version,* © 1973, 1978, 1984 by International Bible Society. All rights reserved. Used by permission of Zondervan Bible Publishers.

Printed in the United States of America

Rehoboth Publishing
P.O. Box 33
Berrien Springs, MI 49103

For additional books, email: ruthvenroy@gmail.com, or visit:
www.rjrbooks.com, or networkdiscipling.org

In Dedication

to

All God's children—"born" and "born-again"

Table of Contents

Acknowledgments VII

Introduction IX

1. Born Before Born-again 15

2. Born: The Adam Effect 23

3. Born Again: The Jesus Factor 43

4. Born Again: Understanding the New "Me" 65

5. Born Again: Renewing My Thinking 99

6. Born Again: Living Christ's Life 129

7. Born Again: The Fullness 165

Conclusion 185

Acknowledgment

THANK YOU!

Dear heavenly Father, precious Savior, and abiding Counselor and Guide.

Lyris, Charisa, Lyrisa and Mirisa—God's personal gifts to me.

Emmerson, Ermine, Patricia and the Network Discipling Ministries family.

I am deeply indebted to ALL of you for your gracious support and valuable contributions towards the production of this priceless treasure.

Introduction

Way back in eternity, before the foundation of the earth was laid and mankind was created, God chose a holy, blameless life in Christ for everyone born into this world, through the lineage of Adam. In accordance with His divine foreknowledge, the Almighty made this redemptive provision as His anticipatory response to the eventuality of sin and human depravity. In this response, He gave the opportunity to every child of sinful Adam to be born again—to literally start over—through the righteous life of Jesus Christ, God's Messiah and Savior of the world.

However, many who have chosen God's option to be born again in Jesus Christ, continue to be confused about what really constitutes born-again life. Consequently, many talk about a life that they have yet to experience, while others frustratingly stumble and fumble along, hoping to capture that life one of these days. For the most part, the born-again life has eluded them, and many have grown to accept the modifications of their Adam self, and/or their adherence to the expectations of their religious community, as what forms the authentic, born-again experience.

In this book, we will seek to expose, depose and even enlarge upon some of the traditional views of what it means to be born again. Some of these are:

❖ To be baptized.
❖ To become a Christian.
❖ To live for God or Jesus Christ.
❖ To change my behavior or lifestyle.
❖ To accept Christ.
❖ To turn my back on the world.
❖ To become a more spiritual person.

To be sure, these views may contain some element of truth with regard to the born-again experience, but they are vague generalities that do not present a comprehensive picture. There is great need for clarification and amplification in order to bring about a more complete understanding. Without this, the above beliefs may become mere "window dressings" for satanic deception. For example, a person who believes being born-again means to become more spiritually inclined, may rigorously pursue religious rituals in order to achieve that end, but will never be born of God through those means. While born-again life may foster spiritual exercises, it is not attained through spiritual pursuits.

This life is neither created by actions of the human will nor its ceaseless striving after "goodness" or "holiness": No, not at all! "Fixing" and "dressing up" the same old man may change his behavior, but does not bring new life to him. Authentic, born-again life is the gracious gift of God, received ONLY through faith in Jesus Christ. What that really means, and how that affects the life-pracice of the person who chooses to believe in Jesus, is the major theme and conversation of this book. Therefore, it is important for readers to examine very closely the Biblical principles presented in this text to have a clearer understanding of this invaluable experience.

To assist in this process, the author has underlined many sections of quoted scriptures to help readers to connect with points under discussion. As an additional aid, some key concepts and scriptures are repeated throughout the manuscript. The author deemed this very necessary, simply because it is too easy for the believer to succumb to what is so very familiar in his natural life that he forgets, or even ignores, key elements and principles of his born-again identity. Renewing the mind of the believer is a work of literary (Word) repetition and living practice; so keeping these vital concepts of spirit-life before him is necessary for nurturing and strengthening his born-again mind-set. Another reason for the repetition is to maintain the connectivity in this born-again dialogue as we move from one chapter to the next.

Fruit that remains

In one of His discourses with His disciples, Jesus said, *"You did not choose Me but I chose you, and appointed you that you would go and bear fruit, and that your fruit would remain*. . . (John 15:16). This straightforward declaration does not speak only the Master's purpose for calling and empowering His disciples; it also reflects the Father's heart towards all those who are born again to new life in His Son. God desires the fruit of the born-again life to remain in every believer, and that all believers will, in turn, work with Him to bear additional fruits by bringing more of His estranged children into this wonderful new life. Jesus expressed this very idea in an earlier verse of the same chapter: "*My Father is glorified by this, that you bear much fruit, and so prove to be My disciples* (John 15:8).

This book is truly about showing how being born-again can be an enjoyable, meaningful, sustainable experience to anyone who believes. It speaks with clarity and certainty about how to be born again without any regrets, and without any desire to turn back. So many who once embraced this life but later turned away from it, did so without even realizing that they had (and still have) what it takes to enjoy and complete it—JESUS. If you are there or anywhere near there, this ONE'S for you. This is your book of hope—a hope that will not fall short of your expectation. Please take the time to study it and share the contents with someone else. Let's fill the world with the good news and unfailing hope.

In conclusion, the author believes that this book will bless the body of Christ abundantly, by adding a greater measure of clarity to the understanding of the one unique experience that makes every believer an integral member in the family of God.

Addendum:
In this book, the absence of capitalization of all aliases and titles referring to the devil has been deliberate, so as not to give undue honorable mention or authority to the arch-deceiver who is bent on the destruction of God's family.

Jesus answered and said to him, *"truly truly, I say to you, unless one is born again, he cannot see the kingdom of God."*

John 3:3, NASB

Chapter 1

BORN:
BEFORE BORN AGAIN

The main scripture for this chapter formed part of a very important conversation Jesus had with a prominent religious leader of His day. The Savior understood very clearly Nicodemus' desperate hunger for peace and the assurance of salvation. While his religious pride drove Nicodemus to skirt around his pressing need, Jesus saved him the trouble by answering the unspoken request of his heart with the very decisive statement: "... *unless a person is born again, he cannot see the kingdom of God* "(John 3:3).

Obviously, from the stand-point of the Savior of the world, to be born again is a very necessary kingdom experience. He said, without it no one can see or enter (John 3:3, 5) the kingdom of God—that is, the kingdom life. Therefore, it is critically important for all kingdom citizens and kingdom prospects to truly understand what this unique, supernatural event is all about.

Truth Nugget #1: *"Born again" implies that some type of birth previously occurred.*

For a person to be born again, that person must have been born sometime in the past. This first birth is what the

Word of God calls natural or flesh birth, the one that originates from the lineage of Adam through our physical birth-parents. The second is what the Bible refers to as divine or spirit birth, the one that originates from Christ through our spiritual birth-parents—the Holy Spirit and the Word of God. Here is a simple illustration of this truth:

Born => Natural or "flesh and blood" birth
Born-again => Divine or Spirit birth

These are the two birthing processes that Jesus pointed out to Nicodemus on the night when this Jewish leader sought His counsel. Further, these two experiences serve as reference points for all those who, like Nicodemus, are seeking eternal life in the kingdom of heaven. Jesus said: "*That which born of the flesh is flesh, and that which is born of the Spirit is spirit*" (John 3:6, emphasis mine).

It is very important for us to understand that Jesus did not say that that which is born of the Spirit is **spiritual**, but that it is **spirit.** There is a big difference between the two. **Spirit** points to existence or what the person or thing is; whereas **spiritual** describes nature or how that person or thing behaves or functions. However, these two elements of the born-again experience—spirit and spiritual—will be dealt with further a little later. Nevertheless, whatever is born of the Spirit is not flesh or natural, but spirit or divine. A dog cannot give birth to a cat, or a pig a horse. In the same way, whatever is born again of the Spirit of God cannot be flesh.

Truth Nugget #2: *There could be no birth without pre-existence.*

In the natural realm, a person must first exist as a fetus before he can be born into this world. Now, if we should extend this truth backward, that person must first exist as a seed-life (sperm) in his father, waiting for the appropriate mother and time to provide the opportunity and environment for that seed to take root—that is, conception—and

Whatever is born of the Spirit is not flesh or natural, but spirit or divine.

grow. Unless these occur, it is totally impossible for that sperm (seed) to become an embryo, and eventually be born into the world as a viable human being.

When we project this truth of pre-existence thousands of generations backwards, we understand that all naturally born human beings had their pre-existence in the seeds of the first man, Adam. Further, we must not forget that even though Adam needed Eve in order to "father" children into this world, Eve also came from a rib taken from him. Thus, Adam is really the father of all humanity— male and female species.

Truth Nugget #3: *Pre-existence does not guarantee birth or safe, healthy delivery into this world.*

Although all men carry seeds of potential human beings in themselves, if those seeds never leave their bodies to find the fertile wombs of the mothers appointed to bear them, they will never be born into this world. While a single emission of semen contains millions of egg-seeking sperms, it takes only one sperm to win the fight to penetrate that egg and start the life cycle of another human being. The remaining millions of potential candidates die without a trace. Their existence did not guarantee the completion of their mission to become a fetus in a woman's womb, and later, a living being in the world.

Beside this "life-or-death" sperm fertilization race, there are many other adverse elements that can pose serious threat to the life of a developing fetus, reducing its chance to exit the womb as a newborn baby. Quite often, a pregnant woman never gives careful consideration to her pre-natal risks until she encounters severe complications with her pregnancy. Some women have experienced great pain and devastating losses through pregnancy miscarriages. It took many of them several attempts and patient bed-rest before they gave birth to living infants.

Moreover, the infant's traumatic journey to life through the vaginal passage is nothing short of a miraculous gift of God. Although the distance from the womb to the outside world averages less than a foot, it is fraught with many dangers, which often make giving birth a very long, harrowing experience. Additionally, the staggering increase of embryonic research and of unwanted and abnormal pregnancies are always very clear and present dangers that diminish the likelihood of a baby making it to the outside world.

Consequently, whatever the nature of an individual's pre-existence before birth, there is absolutely no guarantee that he/she will experience a successful natural, healthy delivery into the world. However, the truth remains that all of humanity pre-existed in the first man, Adam, before anyone was ever born into this world. In the very same way, through God's perfect plan of redemption, all of humanity has a spiritual pre-existence in Jesus Christ, giving all the opportunity to be born again into the eternal kingdom of heaven.

These two very important truths about humanity's pre-existence are of vital significance to the following conversation in this book. Therefore, critical elements pertaining to both of them will be explained throughout this manuscript, in order to provide readers with a clearer understanding of the born-again experience.

Truth Nuggets Summary

1. *Born again implies that some type of birth previously occurred.*

2. *There could be no birth without pre-existence.*

3. *Pre-existence does not guarantee birth or safe, healthy delivery into this world.*

*Therefore, just as through one man [Adam]
sin entered into the world, and death through
sin, and so <u>death spread to all me, because all
sinned</u>.*

Romans 5:12, bracket mine

Chapter 2

BORN:
THE ADAM EFFECT

As the head of the human race and ruler over all creation, Adam's rise and fall have influenced the birth, existence and experience of every person born into the world. When the father of humanity sinned against his Creator, he did not only imperil his life and future, but also the life of all future generations. The Bible states very clearly,

> *Therefore, just as through one man sin entered into the world, and death through sin, and so <u>death spread to all men, because all sinned</u>.*

> Romans 5:12

In Adam <u>all die</u>. . . 1 Corinthians 15:22

Truth Nugget #1: *When Adam sinned, all humanity sinned with him, because all humanity was embedded in the seed of his loins.*

Adam's decision to obey the devil through the voice of his wife, virtually sold the human race into a life of slavery to sin and rebellion against God. The apostle Paul confirmed this truth when he expressed his frustration with his life before knowing Christ as Messiah, Savior and Lord.

> *We know that the Law is spiritual; but I am a creature of the flesh [carnal, unspiritual], <u>having been sold</u> into slavery under [the control of] sin.*

Romans 7:14, AMP

Before we were even born into this world, we were bound by *the law of sin and death* that was already at work in our nature, through the corrupt seed of our forefather, Adam.

> *For I joyfully concur with the <u>law of God</u> in the inner man, [23]but I see <u>a different law in the members of my body</u>, waging war against the law of my mind and making me a prisoner of <u>the law of sin which is in my members</u>.*

Romans 7:22, 23

Consequently, all humanity has committed sin because we are "natural-born" sinners, and we do not become sinners based on the sins we commit. In other words, it is the sinner that produces the sinful behavior and not sinful behavior that turns the person into a sinner. Our noblest attempts to obey God's law are always undermined by the law (principle) of sin, naturally ingrained in our mind and members of our body. This reminds me of a story I once heard from a former Bible professor and evangelist:

A scorpion desperately wanted to get across a very wide river. He spotted a turtle on the river's edge just ahead of him. He quickly approached the docile creature and asked her very politely to allow him the privilege to ride on her sturdy back to the other side. The wise turtle said very kindly, "I am sorry Mr. Scorpion, I would have gladly taken you across, but I am afraid of your poisonous sting." "You may kill me in the middle of our swim over this river." "Nonsense, Mrs. Turtle," replied Mr. Scorpion. "If I should sting you in the middle of our swim, you will not only die, but I would certainly drown; and I definitely do not want die."

The wise, old turtle thought for a little while, and then she said: "Alright, you had me fooled for a moment, but you have a very valid point; drowning is no fun at all." "Come on, hop aboard, and I'll gladly take you over." The scorpion got unto the back of the turtle and they began their journey over the river. Sure enough, when they got a little more than mid-stream, the scorpion jumped on the unprotected head of the turtle and delivered its venomous sting. The turtle gave a very loud "squawk" and in its dying breath said: "Mr. Scorpion you deceived me; now we are both going to die." The scorpion replied sadly, "I am terribly sorry Mrs. Turtle, I tried very hard not to harm you, but it is just my nature to sting. It's what I was made to do!"

Like "Mr. Scorpion," it is the nature of Adam's descendants to commit sin; it is what we were born to do. We were born in sin and fashioned in iniquity (Psalm 51:5).

All humanity commits sin because we are natural-born sinners.

Adam's deadly seed of lust and corruption lies incubated in the body and soul of the "innocent" newborn, and insidiously permeates and influences the life of the growing infant. The Word of God reveals that *the wicked go astray from the womb; they err from their birth, speaking lies* (Psalm 58:3). No one has to teach a toddler how to manipulate its parents, or a young child how to lie to escape discipline. The death-dealing sin virus clings to its host from conception in the womb till the end of it life. Yes! From beginning to end, sin and humanity are inseparable. The Bible confirms that *all have sinned and come short of the glory of God* (Romans 3:23); and that *there is none righteous, no, not one* (Romans 3:10).

Alienation from God

The most far-reaching effect of Adam's sin is that it

separated humanity from the life and light of God. The result of that separation was a life totally opposite to who God is and what He represents. The Holy Scriptures indicate very clearly that *God is light, and in Him there is no darkness at all* (1 John 1:5). The eternal God is also the Originator of ALL life, and life apart from Him can only lead to death and decay.

Paradoxically, the Bible refers to this life of separation from God as one that is *dead in transgression and sin* (Ephesians 2:1). In other words, from God's perspective, a person who is living a life without any meaningful reference to His moral authority over him, is, for all spiritual and eternal purposes, really dead while he lives on the earth. That person is dead to his true condition before God; dead to the salvation that God has provided for him in Jesus Christ; and completely oblivious to all God is doing in his life and in the world, to lead him in the direction of eternal life through Christ.

Truth Nugget #2: *Humanity's alienation from God has given the race a false sense of reality, and a corrupt understanding of morality and evil.*

The apostle Paul gives us a very colorful "clip" of what characterizes a life that is alienated from God in the following passage of scripture:

So I tell you this, and insist on it in the Lord, that you must no longer live as the Gentiles do, in the futility of their thinking. [18]They are darkened in their understanding and separated from the life of God because of the ignorance that is in them due to the hardening of their hearts. [19]Having lost all sensitivity, they have given themselves over to sensuality so as to indulge in every kind of impurity, with a continual lust for more.

Ephesians 4:17-19

Some observers may consider this a very troubling portrayal of fallen humanity, yet this picture is what is so very typical of our modern secular society. Human beings seem to have lost all sense of moral direction, being swept away in the raging seas of hatred, crime, violence, drunkenness, sensuality and un-godly acts of every description.

However, such moral and social depravity is the direct result of the *vain thinking, darkened understanding,* and *hardened hearts* that emerge as the fallout of humanity's alienation from the life of God. In this regard, Paul gives a more comprehensive, jaw-dropping depiction of estranged humanity in **Romans 1:18-32** that is worthy of our prayerful review.

¹⁸*For the wrath of God is revealed from heaven against all ungodliness and unrighteousness of men <u>who suppress the truth in unrighteousness</u>, ¹⁹because <u>that which is known about God is evident within them</u>; for <u>God made it evident to them</u>. ²⁰For since the creation of the world His invisible attributes, His eternal power and divine nature, have been clearly seen, being understood through what has been made, so that <u>they are without excuse</u>.*

²¹*For even though they knew God, they did not honor Him as God or give thanks, but they became futile in their speculations, and <u>their foolish heart was darkened</u>. ²²<u>Professing to be wise, they became fools</u>, ²³and <u>exchanged the glory of the incorruptible God for an image in the form of corruptible man</u> and of birds and four-footed animals and crawling creatures.*

²⁴*Therefore God gave them over in the lusts of their hearts to impurity, so that their bodies would be dishonored among them. ²⁵For <u>they exchanged the truth of God for a lie</u>, and <u>worshiped and served the creature rather than the Creator</u>, who is blessed*

forever. Amen.

[26]For this reason <u>God gave them over to degrading passions</u>; for <u>their women exchanged the natural function for that which is unnatural</u>, [27]and <u>in the same way also the men abandoned the natural function of the woman and burned in their desire toward one another</u>, <u>men with men committing indecent acts and receiving in their own persons the due penalty of their error</u>.

[28]And <u>just as they did not see fit to acknowledge God any longer</u>, <u>God gave them over to a depraved mind, to do those things which are not proper</u>, [29]being filled with all unrighteousness, wickedness, greed, evil; full of envy, murder, strife, deceit, malice; they are gossips, [30]slanderers, haters of God, insolent, arrogant, boastful, inventors of evil, disobedient to parents, [31]without understanding, untrustworthy, unloving, unmerciful; [32]and <u>although they know the ordinance of God</u>, that those who practice such things are worthy of death, <u>they not only do the same, but also give hearty approval to those who practice them</u>.

There is absolutely no doubt that modern humanity is living right in the middle of this uncompromising prophetic Word of God. Here is a clear summary of the above scripture:

1. **See verses 18-20.** People live in denial by suppressing the truth about God and morality, in their attempt to silence God's witness against their corrupt behavior. Is there any wonder then why electronic media and conventional "wisdom" try so very hard to squeeze God out of every public conversation? But the Holy Scriptures say that they are without excuse because of God's un-erasable, internal witness against them through the voice of their conscience.

2. **See verses 21-23.** In order to pursue their futile speculations, immoral people willfully and unashamedly refuse to include God in their thoughts and conversations. Instead, they give more recognition and glory to their kind and to their foolish "wisdom" concerning their lifestyle.

3. **See verses 24-32.** Because of their rejection of His moral authority, God allows the ungodly to follow their immoral lusts and permits their sinful behaviors to run their course to their devastating end. Consequently, we are experiencing today an increasing manifestation of vicious hatred and evil

in our world, and of an intense surge of unnatural human affection—men with men, women with women. What was once considered to be a dark, covert, "closet" phenomenon is now openly declared as acceptable, while its conspirators try desperately to force the God of light into a "closet" of "forgettable" darkness.

Every fabric of modern society is reeling under the growing influence of the gay and lesbian movement and their demand for a re-definition of the marriage institution. The same-sex marriage agenda has force its way into the religious community and is seriously testing the integrity and moral resolve of what was once regarded as society's conscience—the Church. Church leaders are now compelled to negotiate a position of compromise to accommodate the fleshly demands of these spiritually blinded victims of the evil one.

Interestingly, the Word of God confirms that if the truth of the gospel is hidden, it is hidden to those who are perishing, *in whose case the god of this world [satan] has blinded the minds of the unbelieving so that they might not see the light of the gospel of the glory of Christ, who is the image of God* (2 Corinthians 4:3-4)

Moreover, those who advocate the same-sex

lifestyle by utilizing the power of electronic media, celebrity "out-of-the-closet" disclosures, political funding and the "worldly-wise" intelligentsia to endorse and promote their agendas, are completely clueless to the fact that they are operating contrary to merciful will of God, whose judgment against sin and evil is an uncomfortable certainty.

Doomed for Destruction

For the wages of sin is death . . . Romans 6:23

Truth Nugget #3: *Humanity cannot change itself or its course towards eternal destruction without deliverance from heaven.*

Because of Adam's sin, life on planet earth became a slow, painful, death-march to eternal destruction; and humanity can neither change itself nor its destructive course without divine help. The Bible confirms that all the living know that they shall die (Ecclesiastes 9:5). However, the ultimate effect of Adam's deadly misstep at the dawn of Creation is the two un-avoidable appointments it has imposed upon all his descendants—death and judgment regarding our eternal destiny.

And as it is appointed unto men once to die,
but after this the judgment:

Hebrews 9:27

With all its noblest intentions, intelligence and creativity, human-kind is totally powerless to handle the sin problem, along with its natural or eternal consequences. A man's best effort to change himself is an act in total futility and frustration. Through His prophet Jeremiah, God asked and answered the very poignant question: *Can the Ethiopian change his skin or the leopard its spots? Neither can you do good who are accustomed to doing evil* (Jeremiah 13:23, NIV). Understanding the plight of man's condition before God, the prophet uttered the plaintive plea:

> *O LORD, I know that the way of man is not in himself: it is not in man that walketh to direct his steps. 24O LORD, correct me, but with judgment; not in thine anger, lest thou bring me to nothing.*

Jeremiah 10:23, 24

Additionally, the Holy Scriptures affirm that *there is a way that seems right to a man, but in the end it leads to death* (Proverbs 16:25, NIV). The apostle Paul expressed this frustration before he experienced the power of the living Christ in his life.

> *For we know that the Law is spiritual, but I am of flesh, sold into bondage to sin. ¹⁵<u>For what I am doing, I do not understand; for I am not practicing what I would like to do, but I am doing the very thing I hate</u>. ¹⁶But if I do the very thing I do not want to do, I agree with the Law, confessing that the Law is good. ¹⁷So now, <u>no longer am I the one doing it, but sin which dwells in me</u>. ¹⁸For I know that nothing good dwells in me, that is, in my flesh; <u>for the willing is present in me</u>, <u>but the doing of the good is not</u>.*
>
> *¹⁹<u>For the good that I want, I do not do, but I practice the very evil that I do not want</u>. ²⁰But if I am doing the very thing I do not want, <u>I am no longer the one doing it</u>, <u>but sin which dwells in me</u>. ²¹I find then the principle that evil is present in me, the one who wants to do good. ²²For I joyfully concur with the law of God in the inner man, ²³but <u>I see a different law in the members of my body, waging war</u>*

> *against the law of my mind and making me a*
> *prisoner of the law of sin which is in my*
> *members*.

> [24]*Wretched man that I am! Who will set me*
> *free from the body of this death?*

Romans 7:14-24

What Paul describes in the above scriptural verses is the utter human helplessness in dealing with the sin condition—the never-ending, ever-losing battle between a person's will to do good, and the resident sin that drives him to do evil instead. This stupor-like experience often leaves the sinner in a state of puzzling defeat and helpless resignation to the cravings of his sinful nature.

One Way Out

> *For God so loved the world, that he gave his*
> *only begotten Son, that whosoever believeth*
> *in him should not perish, but have everlasting*
> *life.*

John 3:16, KJV

Although the effects of Adam's transgression are great and far-reaching, the love and mercy of God exceed them far beyond measure; for where sin abounds grace abounds even the more (Romans 5:20). Sin can never exhaust the super-abounding grace of God. The Bible says that *God demonstrates His own love toward us, in that while we were yet sinners, Christ died for us* (Romans 5:8). Sin, while threatening impending doom upon humanity, is never a threat to God's overflowing grace. God knew that humanity could do absolutely nothing to save itself from its terrible fate, so He made the first move toward the sinful race, extending Himself in Christ to redeem the world.

> *Sin can never exhaust the super-abounding grace of God.*

> *Now all these things are from <u>God</u>, who <u>reconciled us to Himself through Christ</u> and gave us the ministry of reconciliation, [19]namely, that <u>God was in Christ reconciling the world to Himself</u>, not counting their trespasses against them, and He has committed to us the word of reconciliation.*

> 2 Corinthians 5:18, 19

The great truth about salvation is that through His life

and in His death, God was in Christ, reconciling (making peace with) the world to Himself. In His Son, Jesus Christ, God offered to the fallen world the ONLY door to salvation and peace.

> *"And there is salvation in no one else; for there is <u>no other name under heaven</u> that has been given among men by which we must be saved."*

Acts 4:12

It was Jesus, Himself, who once said: "<u>*I am the door*</u>, *if anyone enters through Me, he will be saved, and shall go in and out and find pasture*" (John 10:9). He also said: "<u>*I am the way*</u>, *and the truth, and the life, <u>no one</u> comes to the Father but through Me*" (John 14:6). Christ is the only door and the only way to salvation for all Adam's children.

Truth Nugget #4: *The ONLY way out of humanity's hell-bound dilemma is through God's total recall of the Adam-man and his complete replacement by the Christ-man.*

This completely new make-over presents no other alternative for humanity's redemption. It is the only choice available to the lost race. No physical or behavioral modification, or intellectual upgrade of the Adam-man, is of any value to his salvation. Absolutely nothing of the old in the BEST of humanity is of the slightest good for God's use, for nothing pertaining to flesh (or natural life) could ever please the Almighty (Romans 8:8). God's plan entails making everything new in the perfect life of Christ. Much more concerning this will appear later.

However, the divine miracle by which God's redemptive do-over is executed is called the "new birth" or "born-again" experience. The in-coming spirit-life of Jesus, through the Holy Spirit, is humanity's only hope to bring the race out of a life of sin, condemnation and eternal death, into an endless life of righteousness, justification and eternal peace.

> . . . *For if by the transgression of the one [Adam] the many died, much more did the grace of God and the gift by the grace of the one Man, Jesus Christ, abound to the many . . . [17]For if by the transgression of the one [Adam], death reigned through the one [Adam], much more those who receive the abundance of grace and of the gift of righteousness will reign in life through the One, Jesus Christ.*

> Romans 5:15, 17, brackets mine

The rest of this volume will deal with this "new birth" experience, what it really is, how it is achieved and what the "born-again" life really looks like. So keep reading . . .

Truth Nuggets Summary

1. *When Adam sinned, all humanity sinned with him, because all humanity was embedded in the seed of his loins.*

2. *Humanity's alienation from God has given the race a false sense of reality and a corrupt understanding of morality and evil.*

3. *Humanity cannot change itself or its course towards eternal destruction without deliverance from heaven.*

4. *The ONLY way out of humanity's hell-bound dilemma is through God's total recall of the Adam-man and his complete replacement by the Christ-man.*

Blessed be the God and Father of our Lord Jesus Christ, who <u>has blessed</u> us with <u>every spiritual blessing</u> <u>in the heavenly places</u> <u>in Christ</u>, just as <u>He chose us</u> <u>in Him</u> <u>before the foundation of the world</u>, that we should be holy and blameless before Him in love.

Ephesians 1:3, 4

Chapter 3

BORN AGAIN:
THE JESUS FACTOR

We have already seen that a person must first pre-exist as a seed-life in his/her father—and, by backward projection, in Adam—in order to be born into the natural realm. The same is also true in the spiritual realm. A person must first pre-exist in Christ before he/she can be born again (of spirit life) into his/her eternal existence in the kingdom of heaven.

This divine pre-existence in Christ is the most precious gift of our heavenly Father, and forms the heart of the plan of redemption, which He established in our Savior before the creation of the world. Here is how divine inspiration expresses it in Paul's letter to the believers in Ephesus.

Blessed be the God and Father of our Lord Jesus Christ, who <u>has blessed</u> us with <u>every spiritual blessing</u> <u>in the heavenly places</u> <u>in Christ</u>, just as <u>He chose us</u> <u>in Him</u> <u>before the foundation of the world</u>, that we should be holy and blameless before Him in love.

Ephesians 1:3, 4

Truth Nugget #1: *God chose to give all humanity an eternal, spiritual existence in Christ before the creation of the world, and before our time-bound, natural existence in Adam.*

This gracious provision was made because of God's foreknowledge of Adam's sin and its dreadful judgment upon all his descendants. In other words, God established the plan of eternal redemption in Jesus Christ for every human being born into this world. Teeming millions of earth's inhabitants walk around on this planet totally ignorant of their eternal, spiritual existence in the Son of God. All the while, they stumble along believing that the short time they spend on this earth is the best there is, or can ever hope to be. How terribly wrong they are! Here is God's perspective on current human life:

> *Man born of woman is of few days and full of trouble. [2]He springs up like a flower and withers away; like a fleeting shadow, he does not endure.*

Job 14:1, 2, NIV

What a fitting description of life here on earth—few days, full-of-trouble, flower-life, and disappearing shadow. However, wherever there is a shadow, there must be some form of reality casting it (the shadow). That reality is not what

God established the plan of eternal redemption in Jesus Christ for every human being born into this world.

we see or experience now in this present world. Instead, it was the full, abundant life that Adam experienced before the Fall, and what God provided in Christ for our redemption before this world began. This present life, at its very best, is like a mirage in the desert, a mere chasing after the wind. The wise preacher said:

I have seen all the works which have been done under the sun, and behold, all is vanity and striving after wind.

Ecclesiastes 1:14

There is absolutely no control over, and no permanence to, the present life we have come to know. A person may spend his very short time on this earth trying to accumulate as much as he can, hoping to make his life comfortable and happy in his later years, but may never live to see the years he calls "later". There are just so many adverse variables that nibble away or suddenly devour the results of our labor under the sun, that life is reduced to a game of chance. A person could be living well in a very beautiful home today, and before tomorrow, either that home could be gone—by some unforeseen disaster—or the person, himself, could be no more.

A very dear neighbor of mine lost her home in a fire one night, while she was out of town. Absolutely nothing was saved from what her years of labor provided. Fortunately, the house was insured, and she was able to rebuild her home with a lot more space and amenities than her previous dwelling. However, just when she was getting settled into her new place, she was diagnosed with a life-threatening illness. In less than a year, my dear neighbor and friend passed away.

Here is another illustration of the reality of this life. One Christmas season, a few years ago, I was visiting the country of my birth—Trinidad, West Indies. I was there in time to see our very young, female, international, boxing champion successfully defend her WBC world title. She was ranked as the #1 female light middleweight boxer of all-times, winning all of her 17 title matches, and capably defending her eight world titles six consecutive times.[1] I recall seeing her on local television shaking her right index finger at the camera, while shouting, "number one baby!" That was the night of December 26, 2008. Nine days later, on January 4, 2009, Trinidad and Tobago and the rest of the world woke up to hear the devastating news that Giselle Salandy, the 21 year old boxing sensation, had died from injuries she sustained from a motor vehicle accident that morning.

Indeed, this is the very sad tale of a life gone too

soon—of a rising champion's strife after the wind called life (Ecclesiastes 1:14). Regrettably, all humanity is born into an existence that marches to untimely, but certain, death. There is absolutely no permanence here; only change and decay abound. However, God offers to all the option of a fulfilling, eternal, born-again life in Jesus Christ, the Savior of the world. Jesus expressed this alternative quite clearly when He became flesh and lived amongst us (John 1:14). He said, "*The thief comes only to steal and kill and destroy; I came that they may have life, and have it abundantly*" (John 10:10).

The Redemptive Life of Jesus

For the wages of sin is death, but the free gift of God is eternal life in Christ Jesus our Lord.

Romans 6:23

The entire Bible is a real-life story about the eternal God full of love for a planet in rebellion. It portrays God extending Himself through His Son, Jesus Christ, to secure the redemption and release of His estranged children from the destructive dominion of the devil. The Scriptures affirm that God was operating in His Son, reconciling the lost world to Himself (2 Corinthians 5:18, 19).

Christ came not only to pay the ransom price for the

sin of humanity, but also to provide us with a life that soundly defeated the evil hosts of darkness and the world. The Bible says that He came so that He might destroy the works of the devil (1 John 3:8). Be assured that those works include every facet of the devil's operations upon this planet, and particularly in the lives of Adam's descendants. Read what the Word of God says about this in the book of Hebrews:

> *Therefore, since the children share in flesh and blood, He Himself likewise also partook of the same, that <u>through death He might render powerless him who had the power of death, that is, the devil,</u> [15] and <u>might free those who</u> through fear of death <u>were subject to slavery all their lives</u>.*

Hebrews 2:14, 15

The death of Christ means everything to the believer. It breaks the legal claim of the devil upon the life of all who receive Christ as their Savior and Lord. However, it is His resurrected life that delivers the believer from the fear of death and every shackle of satanic servitude. The Bible states that Christ *tasted death for everyone* (Hebrews

> *The death of Christ . . . breaks the legal claim of the devil upon the life of all who receive Christ as their Savior and Lord.*

48

2:9), and *having concluded this, that <u>one died for all,</u> <u>therefore all died</u>;* [15]*and He [Christ] died for all, so that they who live might <u>no longer live for themselves</u>, but <u>for Him who died and rose again on their behalf</u>* (2 Corinthians 5:14, 15).

Our Baptism

Christ did not only die for us; He died as us. When He died, we died—our baptism testifies of this death. When He arose, so did we in Him. It is Christ's resurrected life that releases us from our Adam connection (all the laws, physical and spiritual, that bind us to him—**See Romans 7:1-6**), and unites us with Him through our born-again spirit existence in Him. The Word of God says that anyone who is joined to Christ through baptism has not only clothed himself with Christ (Galatians 3:27), but that he is also one spirit with Him (1 Corinthians 6:17). This is our permanent new union. What, therefore, God has joined together, no power on earth or in hell can part asunder, because the state of this union is exceedingly strong! Listen to the Word of God:

> *What shall we then say to these things? If God be for us, who can be against us?* [32]*He that spared not his own Son, but delivered him up for us all,* *how shall he not with him also freely give us all things?*

[33]*Who shall lay anything to the charge of God's elect?* <u>It is God that justifieth</u>.

[34]**Who is he that condemneth?** <u>It is Christ that died</u>, yea rather, <u>that is risen again</u>, <u>who is even at the right hand of God</u>, <u>who also maketh intercession for us</u>.

[35]*Who shall separate us from the love of Christ?* Shall tribulation, or distress, or persecution, or famine, or nakedness, or peril, or sword? [36]As <u>it is written</u>, For thy sake we are killed all the day long; we are accounted as sheep for the slaughter. [37]Nay, <u>in all these things we are more than conquerors through him that loved us</u>.

[38]*For <u>I am persuaded</u>, that neither death, nor life, nor angels, nor principalities, nor powers, nor things present, nor things to come, [39]Nor height, nor depth, nor any other creature, shall be able to separate us from the love of God, which is in Christ Jesus our Lord.*

Romans 8:31-39, KJV

In this new union, the child of God is under the loving care and protection of his one-spirit spouse, Jesus Christ. The above scripture highlights this fact by posing six powerful, rhetorical questions—namely, (1) *What shall we then say to these things?* (2) *If God be for us, who can be against us?* (3)

> *Christ did not only die for us; He died as us. When He died, we died.*

He that spared not his own Son, but delivered him up for us all, how shall he not with him also freely give us all things? (4) *Who shall lay anything to the charge of God's elect?* (5) *Who is he that condemneth?* (6) *Who shall separate us from the love of Christ?*

The implied answers to all these questions point to one indisputable truth—the Father stands in total defense and justification of all those who choose to join themselves to His Son. The state of that union is so strong and indestructible that there is absolutely NOTHING in ALL creation that is able to break or change it, except the believer's willful choice to divorce himself completely from Christ. More will be said about this later.

Truth Nugget #2: *Christ's life is just as important as His death. His death paid the price for sin; His life gives us victory over satan, sin and the grave.*

For if while we were enemies we were

reconciled to God through the death of His Son, much more, having been reconciled, <u>we shall be saved by His life</u>.

Romans 5:10

According to the above scripture, we are really saved by Christ's victorious, resurrected life. If the Savior did not rise from the dead, then His death would have been useless, and we would still be dead in our sins. Paul testifies that such a scenario will make our preaching of the gospel worthless, our faith in Christ useless, and our lives the most miserable of all humanity (1 Corinthians 15:14-19). However, we must give thanks to God continually for Christ's resurrected life, by which our victory over sin's dominion and our hope of eternal life are guaranteed.

The state of the union between Christ and believers is so strong . . . that there is absolutely NOTHING in ALL creation that is able to break or change it.

Our legacy is resurrected Life, which has made, and can still make, the sick well and the diseased healed; the blind to see and the lame to walk; the deaf to hear and the dumb to speak; the dead raise to life; and the prisoner of addiction, sin and guilt completely free. This is the Life we received when we were born again of the Spirit of God. Indeed we are saved by the operation of His life within us, and not by the fleshly strivings of our well-intentioned souls.

In His conversation with Nicodemus, the Savior made it absolutely clear that unless a person is born again he cannot experience eternal life in the kingdom of God. Jesus said that every kingdom-seeker must be born of (1) *of water* — pointing to our baptism, which is symbolic of death and burial of our former natural life, and our resurrection to new life in Christ; and (2) *of the Spirit* — pointing to the birth of new spirit-life of Christ within the believer. Paul wrote:

> "*. . . do you not know that all of us who have been baptized into Christ Jesus have been baptized into His death? ⁴Therefore we have been buried with Him through baptism into death, so that as Christ was raised from the dead through the glory of the Father, so we too might walk in newness of life. ⁵For if we have become united with Him in the likeness of His death, certainly we shall also be in the likeness of His resurrection, ⁶knowing this, that our old self was crucified with Him, in order that our body of sin might be done away with, so that we would no longer be slaves to sin.*"

Romans 6:1-6

Through baptism, the believer mirrors both the death (the penalty for sin) and the resurrection (victorious, endless life) of Jesus Christ—the inseparable acts of Christ's life that bring complete redemption to all who believe in Him. However, the Holy Spirit is the Divine Agent that regenerates the life of Jesus within the believer at the moment he receives Jesus as his Savior and Lord. It is through His influence in the believer's spirit (Romans 8:16) that the child of God is able to live the resurrected life of Jesus.

Truth Nugget #3: *Born-again life is the incorruptible "seed" of the resurrected, victorious life of Jesus.*

God's Choice

The gift of eternal life in Jesus is what God chose for every human being before the world began. This gift of Christ to mankind and the world was the cornerstone of the plan of redemption. Our salvation is never predicated upon any action on our part, nor upon our affiliation with any type of religious organization. It is based entirely upon the authoritative choice of the omniscient God, made way back in eternity (Ephesians 1:3, 4).

In Romans 8:29, the Bible says that *those whom He [God] foreknew, He also predestined [pre-determined or determined beforehand] to become conformed to the image of His Son, so that He would be the firstborn among many brethren* (Romans 8:29, brackets mine). Through His divine foreknowledge, wisdom and grace, God decided that every one of His born-again children will be created anew in the image of His Son. The total plan of redemption was hinged on God's pre-creation

Our salvation is never predicated upon . . . our affiliation with any type of religious organization.

decisions and the provisions He made available in Jesus Christ.

Just as Adam carried all flesh generations in himself when this world began, so, too, Christ carried all spirit generations in Himself long before Adam was even created. Without any dispute, Christ was totally a spirit being—without a natural, human body—before the foundation of the world. A body had to be prepared for Christ before He came into our world (Hebrews 10:5). Now, since Christ prior, eternal state of existence was Spirit, it also holds true that all the generations imbedded in Christ's loins (so to speak) were correspondingly totally spirit—not flesh.

As it is in the natural, so it is also in the spiritual. Although God's plan of redemption made the provision for all humanity to enjoy an embedded pre-existence in Christ before the world was created, that provision did not warranty that all humanity would be born again unto eternal life in the kingdom of God. Unless, and until, this birth takes place, humanity's pre-existent life in Christ cannot become a viable, living entity. In other words, it is only after a person receives Christ, and is born again of the Spirit of God, that his provisional eternal pre-existence in Christ is actually regenerated within him.

How Is A Person Born Again?

> *But as many as received Him to them He gave the right to become children of God, even to those who believe in His name, <u>who were born</u> <u>not of blood</u>, <u>nor of the will of the flesh</u>, <u>nor of the will of man</u>, but <u>of God</u>.*

> John 1:12, 13

> *Being born again, not of corruptible seed, but of incorruptible seed, <u>by the Word of God</u>, which liveth and abideth forever.*

> 1 Peter 1:23, KJV

When we combine these two scriptures, we have a fairly good understanding of how a person is born again— that is, how the life that God chose for him before the foundation of the world (Ephesians 1:3, 4) comes into existence in the spirit realm.

According to the first scripture, whenever an individual receives Christ as his Savior and Lord, that person is said to be born of God, and has the God-given right to call himself a child of God. This is a totally spirit and faith transaction between God and the repentant sinner, based squarely upon the infallible Word of God.

> *No human agent or agency has the authority to cancel God's born-again life in the person who believes in Jesus.*

This act of God giving birth to new life in Christ (not Adam) is completely independent of any type of human interference. Notice the language of the text: *who were born not of blood, nor of the will of the flesh, nor of the will of man, but of God* (John 1:13). No human agent or agency has the authority or power to intercept or cancel God's born-again life in the person who believes in Jesus. This is a right that God reserves solely to Himself and the believer.

The second scripture provides the perfect explanation of how a person is brought to that favorable place for the first experience to occur. A person cannot attain to the position to receive Christ without the combined witness of the Holy Spirit and the Word of God upon his sinful soul. It is this witness that brings about the birth of the spirit-life of the born-again man.

Truth Nugget #4: *Until the seed of Christ's eternal Spirit connects with the eternal Word of God in the soul of the natural-born individual, his pre-existent life in Jesus will not become a reality.*

Word Mother, God Father

1 Peter 1:23, KJV says that we are *born again not of corruptible seed, but incorruptible seed, by the Word of God, which liveth and abideth forever*. The corruptible seed represents the carnal nature of Adam in our natural life. However, the incorruptible seed is the spirit nature of Jesus that brings new divine life to the spirit of the born-again believer, in his response to the Word of faith.

In human terms, born-again spirit-life is the product of the inseparable union between a God-father and a Word-mother. God, through His eternal Spirit, is the One providing the incorruptible, imperishable spirit-seed of Christ, and the Word of God providing the nurturing environment for the seed-life to take root and grow. Moreover, just as the Spirit (Father) and the Word (Mother) are eternal, the life which they produce and sustain in the believer is also eternal.

In the normal reproduction of human life, the mother that provides the egg for sperm fertilization is also blessed with two milk-producing fountains (breasts) to nourish the life she produces. In the spiritual sense, the Word of God functions in the very same way. It does not only unite with God's Spirit to conceive new life in the believer, but also has two milk-producing fountains in the Old and New Testaments for feeding and nurturing that life. Hence, Peter admonishes every spiritual new-born:

> "... *like newborn babies, long for the pure milk of the word, so that by it you may grow in respect to salvation.*"

> 1 Peter 2:2

It is very important for the born-again child of God to know that reading, studying and meditating on the Word of God must form an integral part of his daily spirit-life if he is to grow in respect to salvation. Just as a new infant cannot survive without constant feeding on the milk provided by its mother, so too, the

Just as the Spirit and the Word are eternal, the life which they produce and sustain in the believer is also eternal.

spirit-life of the believer will be severely disadvantaged if it does not receive sustained nourishment from the eternal Word of God.

Failure by many professed Christians to maintain this daily interaction with the living Word of God is one of the primary reasons for their lack of faith, moral feebleness, spiritual impotence and struggles with sin. Just as mother's milk is naturally endowed with a complete battery of nutrients that promote the healthy growth and development of the infant, the Word of God is divinely designed to provide total nourishment and all-round support to the born-again spirit-life of the believer.

How many believers try to maintain their new life in Christ with only a once-a-week exposure to the Word of God? These do not sense the peril, nor even make any meaningful connection between this unhealthy practice and their less-than-desired lifestyle. The only vivifying agent that has the power to nurture the mind of Christ in the believer's spirit, equipping him with unimaginable spiritual wisdom and insight, is the Word of God. The only way the believer can develop the victorious faith that overcome the world's forces is through hearing, speaking and walking in the living, empowering Word of God.

This Word says that *whatsoever is born of God overcometh the world: and this is the victory that overcometh the world, even our faith* (1 John 5:4, KJV); and that this faith comes by hearing the Word of God (Romans 10:17). It is very important to mention that this Word of God is not a textbook that we retrieve from a dusty shelf, or grab from a counter-top on our way out the door to church. Neither is it a capricious volume for playing "hocus-pocus" life-games with the unseen God. NO! A million times NO!

The Bible is not a textbook for research and information gathering. It is a LifeBook (or Book of Life) that

The Bible is not a textbook . . . It is a LifeBook . . .

provides power, insight and direction for living the abundant life of the redeemed. Moreover, it is *living and active; sharper than any double-edged sword; it penetrates even to dividing soul and spirit, joints and marrow; it judges the thoughts and attitudes of the heart* (Hebrews 4:12, NIV). The book of Proverbs gives this very vital instruction regarding the Word of God:

> *My son, <u>give attention</u> to my words; <u>Incline your ear</u> to my sayings.* [21]*<u>Do not let them depart from your sight</u>; <u>Keep them in the midst of your heart</u>.* [22]*For <u>they are life</u> to those who find them and <u>health to all their body</u>.*

Proverbs 4:20-22

The instruction in the above scripture is very comprehensive and addresses every avenue of influence that feeds the human soul. The Word of God must not only have the full attention of the believer, but must engage his organ of hearing and sight, and form a part of his daily meditation. If the child of God adheres to this counsel with due diligence, he will discover the power in the Word to renew his spiritual, mental and natural life forces.

Further, the Lord Jesus endorses the primacy of the Word of God as the unequalled, life-sustaining agent of human soul. Note the following:

> But He answered and said, "It is written, *'MAN SHALL NOT LIVE ON BREAD ALONE, BUT ON EVERY WORD THAT PROCEEDS OUT OF THE MOUTH OF GOD.'"*

> Matthew 4:4

This declaration does not only hold true for the natural life of man; but this proves even most true for the spirit life of the born-again individual. This is one truth that every child of God must get right every, single day that he lives—the Word of God is the indispensable life-line to the inner-man of his spirit.

Truth-Nuggets Summary

1. *God chose to give all humanity an eternal, spiritual existence in Christ before the creation of the world, and before our time-bound, natural existence in Adam.*

2. *Christ's life is just as important as His death. His death paid the price for sin; His life gives us victory over satan, sin and the grave.*

3. *Born-again life is the incorruptible "seed" of the resurrected, victorious life of Jesus.*

4. *Until the seed of Christ's eternal Spirit connects with the eternal Word of God in the soul of the natural-born individual, his pre-existent life in Jesus will not become a reality.*

Notes:

1. http://en.wikipedia.org/wiki/Giselle_Salandy

Therefore from now on we recognize no one according to the flesh; even though we have known Christ according to the flesh, yet now we know Him in this way no longer.

2 Corinthians 5:16

". . . that which is born of the Spirit is spirit."

John 3:6

Chapter 4

BORN AGAIN:
UNDERSTANDING THE NEW "ME"

*Therefore, if any man <u>be in Christ</u>, he is a new
creature: old things are passed away; behold,
<u>all things</u> are become new.*

2 Corinthians 5:17, KJV

In this chapter we are going to explore elements
pertaining to born-again life. The believer must understand
his true identity in Christ if he or she is to live successfully
the life of the born-again child of God. In the Christian walk,
identity is everything. It is the very root and foundation of
the entire born-again experience. It spells success or failure
in one's dealing with the devil, sin, and all the world's forces.

In over 30 years in pastoral ministry, I have
discovered that many of the professed Christians I have
encountered during that time were very confused about their
true identity in Christ. This is not altogether strange, for even
I was once numbered among them. However, whenever I
would ask the question: "Who are you really?" I would often
be amazed at the similarity of the responses I would receive.
Here are a few examples:

1. "*I am* _____." Most people usually begun by identifying themselves by their name. I would then reply by saying, "Well, that's only your family name, but who are you really?" I often got answers like the following: "Hmmm, I have never really thought about that." "You got me with that one." "You know, that's a really deep question." "I will have to give this some deep thought." "I have never thought about it like that."

2. "*I am a* _____." Other people identified themselves by their religious affiliation. However, when I respond by saying, "That's only your religion, but who are you really?" I usually received some variation of the responses given in #1 above.

3. "*I am a child of God.*" Now, this was my favorite because even if it was an "in the ball-park" or a "politically" correct answer, when I asked, "What do you mean by that?" Most people usually spoke of their religious rituals or practices: "I attend church periodically, read my Bible occasionally, pray every morning and/or evening, fast pretty often," etc. When I asked, "Is this what a child of God really is, or just some of the things you would expect child of God to do?" Again, most people usually go back to responses similar to those in #1 above.

4. Others categorized themselves by their skill, profession, education or job assignment. However, they soon reconsidered their position when they realized that those things only expressed something about themselves, and did not really identify them as individuals.

Identity is Everything

But why is it of such vital importance for an individual to be able to have a very clear understanding of his true identity in this world? Because a person will reflect only who or what he truly perceives himself to be. That is to say, an individual's thought-life and behavior are the direct outgrowths of his perception of his personhood. This truth is very critical to our current discussion since it has an over-arching impact on the quality of the redemptive experience of the born-again believer. Let me illustrate:

Here are two common examples of how many followers of Jesus view their born-again life:

(1) *God does not really expect me to be perfect, because he knows that I am only human.*

This self-centered, self-comforting understanding of one's born-again personhood is far removed from what Jesus expressed in the Word of God: "*Be ye therefore perfect, even*

*Identity is
everything. It is
the very root and
foundation of the
entire born-again
experience.*

as your Father in heaven is perfect" (Matthew 5:48, KJV). Now, it must be that either Jesus is out of touch with our reality, or we are out of touch with what the reality of our life situation really is. Another incredulous scenario would be either Jesus is lying to us, or we just do not know the truth about our life in Him.

Either way, the author of this book believes that it is totally impossible for Jesus to lie, because He is the epitome of all truth and reality, and it is only through Him that what is both truth and reality hold together (Colossians 1:16, 17). Additionally, any human perception that does not conform to the unerring Word of God must be false. It must be then that the above view of the born-again life needs re-evaluation and adjustment to what the Bible defines it to be.

> (2) *Even though I am born again, I will always be a sinner until Jesus returns to put an end to sin.*

This view of born-again life can be called the Siamese twin of the idea expressed in (1) above. It is equally accommodating and debilitating in its effect on the quality of the redemptive experience of the believer, and leads to a person resigning himself to the power of his sinful nature in

Adam—the very nature Christ died to destroy (Romans 6:1-14; 7:1-6; Colossians 2:10, 11). Spiritual mediocrity and a form of godliness without spiritual power (2 Timothy 3:5) become the order of the life characterized by this view of the born-again experience.

Moreover, this misguided perception gives rise to deceptive oxymoron concepts like the "born-again sinner" and "human (flesh) spirituality," also known as being "righteous by works." In the pulpits and in the pews of many religious communities, professed followers of Jesus operate with amazing levels of comfort in these very erroneous zones, which open doors for all types of demonic manifestations to infiltrate the body of Christ under the guise of genuine spiritual experiences.

The truth of the matter is that no one is born again into the kingdom of God a sinner. He may walk around in a body of sin, but the life-treasure of God within that corrupt clay container is no sinner at all, for whosoever is born of God doth not commit sin (1 John 3:9, KJV). More will be said regarding this a little later in this chapter.

Focused Living

Now, if the child of God defines himself totally by his life within, he will reflect the power of that life in his outward behavior. On the other hand, if he continues to define himself by the life of his birth, and not his born-again life within, then he will most certainly reflect all the failures associated with his sinful legacy in Adam. It is that simple. The child of God must remember every moment that he breathes that it is no longer he (Adam self) that lives, but it is the Christ within that now lives and controls his thoughts and life.

> "*I have been crucified with Christ; and it is no longer I who live, but Christ lives in me; and the life which I now live in the flesh I live by faith in the Son of God, who loved me and gave Himself up for me.*"

Galatians 2:20

The "I" of me is gone! The "Christ" in me has come! This must be my focus every moment of every day. I do not live by faith in me, but by faith in the Christ in me. The Christ in me is the truth of who I am, for the "I" of me is dead. However, if I do not know and claim this truth about who I am in Christ, I am left only to live by whoever or whatever I perceive myself to be in Adam. My identity is either in Christ or Adam. There is absolutely no middle-ground! This is the reason it is so important for us to identify who really is this born-again creature in Christ, and to understand what that means to our every-day experience.

The opening scripture for this chapter forms the centerpiece to this discussion. It says that *if any man be in Christ, he is a new creature: old things are passed away; behold, all things are become new* (2 Corinthians 5:17, KJV). The most important truth expressed in this text is that born-again is a *state of being* in Christ—that is, a state of existence, not an idea or paradigm shift in Adam. This state of being is the only qualification for the born-again experience. The word, "if" pre-supposes the binding condition; and the phrase, "in Christ" establishes what that binding condition is. The condition describes a very unique position in, and relation to, God's provision for the salvation of the world, Jesus Christ.

No one in all of the Scriptures uses this "in Christ"[1] expression more than the apostle Paul. Of the 76 times this is recorded in the New Testament of authorized King James Version of the Bible, the gentile apostle used it is 73 times. Through the direct revelation of Jesus Christ (Galatians 1:11, 12; Ephesians 3:1-5), Paul indicates that God

> *Born-again is a state of being in Christ . . . not an idea or paradigm shift in Adam.*

made this "in Christ" provision for all humanity to meet the condition for born-again life. Through this provision, he established all in a distinctive position in Christ before the foundation of the world.

Blessed be the God and Father of our Lord Jesus Christ, who has blessed us with every spiritual blessing in the heavenly places in Christ, ⁴just as <u>He chose us</u> in <u>Him [Christ] before the foundation of the world</u>, that we would be holy and blameless before Him.

Ephesians 1:3, 4

However, this "in Christ" provision holds no guarantee that all will make the choice to benefit from it. Yes, humanity must trust God and make the choice to receive His provision in His Son, in order to be born again into new creatures in Christ Jesus. Permit me to quote again this very important Biblical reminder:

But as many as <u>received Him</u>, to them <u>He gave the right</u> to become children of God, even to <u>those who believe in His name</u>, ¹³who <u>were born</u>, not of blood nor of the will of the flesh nor of the will of man, but <u>of God</u>.

John 1:12, 13

The text indicates quite clearly that the choice to receive Christ—that is, His righteous life and sacrifice—must be made to activate the transaction of the believer's "in Christ" position into born-again life. Only the ones who make this choice have the privilege to be born of God, and the right to call themselves children of the Most High. Those who make this choice are the ones who receive an abundance of grace to overcome the power of their sinful Adam nature, God's free gift of Christ's righteousness as their permanent covering, and the authority to reign in life as joint-heirs of Christ's kingdom.

> *For if by the transgression of the one, death reigned through the one, much more <u>those who receive</u> **the abundance of grace** and of **the gift of righteousness** <u>will reign in life</u> through the One, Jesus Christ.*

Romans 5:17

The Old and the New

Therefore, if any man <u>be in Christ</u>, he is a new creature: old things are passed away; behold, <u>all things</u> are become new.

2 Corinthians 5:17, KJV

Truth Nugget #1: *The born-again spirit-man is a brand new creation from heaven; not an adjustment or improvement of the natural Adam man from earth.*

It is important to note from the above scripture that a person who is "in Christo" — essentially, born again — is an entirely new creation of God. From the perspective of heaven, everything associated with his life in his natural Adam self gives way his new life in his inner spirit-man. His old life has absolutely nothing to offer that would satisfy, even to the smallest degree, his redemptive needs, for ALL its "righteous" actions are filthy rags before God (Isaiah 64:6).

Scary-looking Caterpillars vs Beautiful Butterflies

Caterpillars are strange and scary-looking creatures. At times they can cause a person to have goose bumps just looking at their hairy, jointed body, crawling along some leafy foliage. As a little boy, I hated being near caterpillars, and had often thrown rocks and sticks at them. Never did it cross my mind that these repulsive, creepy creatures, after a little while, converted into beautiful butterflies. I used to chase these transformed critters around in my neighborhood hoping to capture them as my prized possession.

I read recently, that "in order for the change from a caterpillar to a butterfly to take place within the pupa, the caterpillar begins releasing enzymes that literally digest nearly all of its own body. What's left inside the chrysalis is mostly just a very nutrient rich soup from which the butterfly will begin to form."[2] It is reported that in this rich soup lie some neurological elements that hold the vital links connecting the butterfly to the scary-looking caterpillar predecessor.

It is truly amazing that even though a butterfly develops from the gooey remains of a caterpillar, its internal and physical composition and structure—and even its behavior—are totally different from that of a caterpillar. This metamorphic event transforms a weird, crawling, leaf-eating "worm" into a completely new creature—a beautiful, flying, pollen-seeking butterfly.

What a remarkable transformation! And what a powerful illustration of the "born-again" experience of the new creature in Christ Jesus! All the behavior and characteristics of his/her old Adam nature are completely replaced by a new spirit-life from above—the perfect life of Jesus. This is the miracle of God and not the works of man. However, the sad truth is that while the new butterfly believes it can fly, and instinctively does, many born-again believers do not believe they can truly do all things through the Christ-life in them.

Consequently, they continue to live like defeated sinners trying to be saved. They simply do not believe that they can fly (even though some sing about it—"I believe I can fly") like spiritual butterflies, therefore, they continue to crawl like earth-eating "worms". They do not really believe that they are from heaven, so they remain earthbound in their thinking, outlook and experience.

"The 'old' is better"

All Adam's descendants are transgressors by nature, and there is nothing in them that God can put to any good use in the born-again life. This is the one truth that all born-again believers need to understand fully. Far too many born-again children of God are so self-absorbed and deceived by their fleshly endowments that they refuse to believe God's Word. They blindly cling to what their vain imagination tells them about their appearance, intelligence, accomplishments and the deadly remains of the lust of their eyes, lust of their flesh and their worldly pride. This has led many to believe that born-again life has allowance for some measure of blending of the old life with that of the new.

Of course, this is totally contrary to what the Word of God states concerning what God did when He created the born-again individual in Christ—that is, He made ALL things new (2 Corinthians 5:17). The ALL things becoming new does not, in the least, suggests any mixing of the old self with God's new creation. Christ's words to the scribes and Pharisees represent a very clear verification of this misconception.

> *"And no one puts new wine into old wineskins; otherwise the <u>new wine will burst the skins</u> and <u>it will be spilled out</u>, and <u>the skins will be ruined</u>. [38]But <u>new wine must be put into fresh wineskins</u>. [39]And no one, after drinking old wine wishes for new; for he says, 'The old is good enough.'"*

Luke 5:37-39

Although this text had a direct application to the resistant mindset of the Jewish leaders to the teachings of Christ, it also presents a perfect window for viewing the total incompatibility of the "old" natural man and the new creation in Christ. Many who have drunken of the "old" wine of their Adam nature for so long have grown used to the taste. Therefore, their deceptive hearts (Jeremiah 17:9) incite them to believe that the "old" is better than, or if not, just as good as, the "new" wine (spirit-life) that Christ offers.

The apostle Paul encountered this "old wine" mentality among the Jews who stubbornly held on to circumcision of their flesh as the prized element of their identity and religious distinction. For them, a person's Christianity was incomplete unless and until that person was circumcised. In other words, being a new creature was not enough to qualify as a member of their religious community. Circumcision of a man's flesh, not faith in Christ, became the pivotal requirement for anyone seeking salvation and communal fellowship. Paul declared:

> *For neither circumcision nor uncircumcision is anything; but a new creation is everything!*

Galatians 6:15

It is nothing short of amazing to see how this Jewish attitude, which places ritualistic, human behaviors over born-again spirit-life, permeates Christian communities today. Receiving Christ is simply not sufficient! Every religious community has its additional list of human works or rituals that must be met before the salvation-seeker can be accepted fully into the "believing" community.

Many of these communities hang their identity on some prized element in their belief system or religious practice, making faith in Christ alone subservient to the traditions of men. Consequently, born-again believers are forced to conform to religious rules and requirements because church leaders do not trust (or perhaps, because they don't know) what God's grace is doing within these new creatures in Christ.

However, the point made by the apostle Paul is very

clear. Any practice aimed at sanctifying the natural man is absolutely useless. On the other hand, God's new creation—the born-again inner spirit-man—is everything, because he is the object of God's focus. God directs His full attention to the new creation Christ-man, not the old creation Adam-man! His divine grace that provides all the blessings of heaven—including power to resist temptation and overcome sinful behavior—flows in super-abundance only to the believer's inner spirit-man. Hence the reason Paul prayed,

> that He [God] would grant you, according to the riches of His glory, <u>to be strengthened with power through His Spirit in</u> **the inner man**, so that Christ may <u>dwell in your hearts</u> through faith; and that you, being rooted and grounded in love, [18]may be able to comprehend with all the saints what is the breadth and length and height and depth, [19]and to know the love of Christ which surpasses knowledge, that you may be <u>filled up to all the</u> **fullness of God**. [20]Now to Him who is able to do far more abundantly beyond all that we ask or think, according to <u>the power that works</u> **within us.**

Ephesians 3:16-20

The fullness of God is the focus of the life of God within the believer. Whenever professed Christians choose to believe the Word of God, and not be fooled by what they see or think of "the person in the mirror", they will discover the freedom, blessing and influence of the Christ-man within them. But God will not dispense His precious grace to empower or enhance the old wineskin of natural human nature or self-life.

Any practice aimed at sanctifying the natural man is absolutely useless.

It is quite sad that many believers are spiritually and mentally confused regarding who they are in Christ, and what actually transpired when they received Him as Savior and Lord. In essence, they do not have a true comprehension of what being born again really is or means. Consequently, their best efforts to serve the Christ they profess to love are consistently undermined by the aspects of their Adam life which they have not relinquished due to their spiritual ignorance.

Contrary to the Word of God, but to the joy of the archdeceiver, they have professed to have clothed themselves with Christ, but have also made ample provision for their fleshly Adam as well (Romans 13:14). Though their natural Adam flesh remains presently the uncooperative host of their real spirit life, it must be kept under strict discipline by their focused attention on Christ and His life within them.

The Dirt and the Treasure

Another very powerful metaphor that contrasts the "natural man" with the born-again spirit-man is found in Paul's second letter to the Christians living in Corinth.

> *For God, who said, "Light shall shine out of darkness," is the One who has shone in our hearts to give the Light of the knowledge of the glory of God in the face of Christ. ⁷But we have <u>this treasure in earthen vessels</u>, so that <u>the surpassing greatness of the power will be of God</u> and <u>not from ourselves</u>.*

2 Corinthians 4:6, 7

It is quite clear from this scripture that God's supreme interest is in His treasure—the spirit life of Jesus within the believer—and not the earthen vessel of the natural life housing it. The treasure is the Light, and the Light is the knowledge of the glory of God in the face or image of Jesus Christ formed within the believer. God specifically designed it this way, so that the surpassing greatness (or boasting) of the power will only be what God is doing in our spirit, and not what we perceive we are accomplishing through the works of our flesh.

O the depth of the riches both of the wisdom and knowledge of God! How unsearchable are his judgments, and his ways past finding out!

Romans 11:33

Unfortunately, many who spend their days minding dirt miss the presence of God's priceless, born-again, treasure within them. Regrettably, they confuse this "Christ-life within" with their "sanctified" version of their earthen vessels—that is, the good works and behaviors of their natural self-life.

Adam and Christ

Truth Nugget #2: *The born-again spirit-man is a divine creation that is rooted in Christ, the life-giving Spirit.*

Just as being born brings into existence a whole new life in the flesh, being born again gives rise to an entirely new life in the spirit. Being born again is not a supernatural transformation of the natural Adam man. It is the divine creation or regeneration of the spirit-life of Christ within the believer. Therefore, the born-again man is not a flesh being as the sons of Adam, even though he resides in a house of flesh. He is a spirit being, just like the life-giving Spirit that gave birth to him. His origin is from heaven, not of earth.

> So also it is written, "*The first MAN, Adam,*
> *BECAME A LIVING SOUL*." *The last Adam*
> *became a life-giving spirit.* [46]*However, the*
> *spiritual is not first, but the natural; then the*
> *spiritual.* [47]*The first man is from the earth,*
> *earthy; the second man is from heaven.* [48]*As*
> *is the earthy, so also are those who are*
> *earthy; and as is the heavenly, so also are*
> *those who are heavenly.* [49]*Just as we have*
> *borne the image of the earthy, we will also*
> *bear the image of the heavenly.*

1 Corinthians 15:45-49

The above scriptural passage is very interesting because it brings into full view the two heads of two existential states—namely, Adam and Christ. One operates in flesh, the other in spirit. Adam represents the state of existence of every person born into this world; Christ represents the state of existence of every believer born again into the kingdom of heaven—the world to come. Adam is the father of every living soul being; Christ is the Father of every living spirit being.

Just as Adam originated from the earth, so is everyone who is born of him. Just as Christ originated from heaven, so is everyone who is born again of Him. The true citizenship of every born-again believer is heaven, and not the country of his/her natural birth. The Word of God confirms this truth quite clearly: *Our citizenship is in heaven, from which also we eagerly wait for a Savior, the Lord Jesus Christ* (Philippians 3:20).

> *Being born again is not a supernatural transformation of the natural Adam man.*

In Christ's Image

However, the most riveting truth in the above Bible passage is this: Just as we bear the image of Adam in our sinful flesh, so we bear the image of Christ in His righteous spirit-life within us. The born-again spirit-man is created in the likeness of God (Ephesians 4:24) and in the image of Jesus Christ (1 Corinthians 15:49; Colossians 3:10), who is also the exact expression of the heavenly Father (Hebrews 1:3).

Paul also revealed that those who are born again are *God's workmanship, created <u>in Christ Jesus</u> to do good works* . . . (Ephesians 2:10), and that God pre-determined that they would be fashioned in the image of His Son, who was to be the very first model of what they were going to be. The Bible says that *those whom He foreknew, He also predestined to become conformed to the image of His Son, so that He would be the firstborn among many brethren* (Romans 8:29).

Without any doubt, the born-again man is a divine spirit because he was born again of the Divine Spirit—God (John 1:12, 13). Whatever is born of God cannot be flesh, for God is not flesh, but Spirit (John 4:24). Moreover, God's immutable creative law says that every seed must produce after its kind (Genesis 1:11, 12, 21, 24, 25). This new creature in Christ has partaken of divine nature and must believe, think and live under the influence of this mysterious truth.

> . . . *seeing that* <u>*His divine power has granted to us everything pertaining to life and godliness*</u>, *through the true knowledge of Him who called us by His own glory and excellence. ⁴For by these He has granted to us His precious and magnificent promises, so that by them* <u>*you may become partakers of the divine nature*</u>, *having escaped the corruption that is in the world by lust.*

2 Peter 1:3, 4

God has already given His born-again children everything they need for eternal life and godliness in Jesus.

It is the life of Jesus that resides in their inner-man. Whenever they truly believe and live God's great and precious promises, the power of Christ's divine nature will be evident in them. The Bible also says that all God's promises are "yes" and "amen" (final) in Jesus Christ (2 Corinthians 1:20). Therefore, if any man is in Christ, his true nature is spirit and divine, for *as He [Jesus] is, so also are we in this world* (1 John 4:17).

Therefore, it is of critical importance for the born-again believer to see himself as God sees him in Christ (not Adam), and not as what he sees or thinks about himself based on his human perceptions. Paul gave very good counsel regarding this:

> . . . *and He died for all, so that they who live might no longer live for themselves, but for Him who died and rose again on their behalf.* ¹⁶*Therefore <u>from now on we recognize no one according to the flesh</u>; even though we have known Christ according to the flesh, yet now we know Him in this way no longer.*

> 2 Corinthians 5:15, 16

Every born-again believer needs to experience and live the "*from now on*" in this text. He must live in full

Every born-again believer needs to experience and live the "from now on" in 2 Cor. 5:16.

recognition of his spirit existence in Christ, not by what he thinks or feels about the person in the mirror. It is no longer his Adam self that lives or controls his thoughts and life, but Christ who lives in and through him (Galatians 2:20). In the eyes of God, the natural Adam life of every believer is already considered dead, and his real life is hidden with Christ in Him (Colossians 3:3). That is not a position of soul or flesh existence, but one that is totally spirit, for everyone *who joins himself to Lord is <u>one spirit</u> with Him* (1 Corinthians 6:17).

God calls Himself the Father of spirits in contrast to the fathers of our fleshly existence (Hebrews 12:9, 10). It is the born-again spirit life that truly identifies us as God's children (Romans 8:9), and forms the only point of contact through which His every blessing flows to us. It is God's Spirit that bears continuous witness with our spirits, confirming that we are His legitimate children indeed (Romans 8:16).

Born Again Incorruptible

Truth Nugget #3: *Born-again life is not only sinless. It is also sin-proof.*

Being born again, not of corruptible seed, but of incorruptible, by the word of God, which liveth and abideth for ever.

1 Peter 1:23

It is very important to observe that the seed which gives born-again life to the believer is incorruptible. This means, there is absolutely nothing in that seed that is capable of producing decay or death. The only element upon this earth that produces death and decay is sin (Romans 5:12), the very element that embedded corruption in the seed of Adam.

This incorruptible seed, of which Peter speaks in the above text, is nothing other than the Spirit life (1 Corinthians 15:45) of the sinless Son of God that "fathers" the inner-man of the believer's spirit. Moreover, because the last Adam, Jesus Christ, is a sinless, life-giving Spirit (1 Corinthians 15:45), the seeds produced by Him are not only spirit, but sinless as well. Just as the Holy Spirit deposited the sinless, seed life of Jesus into the womb of the Virgin Mary (Luke 1:31-35)—who, by the way, shared Adam's sinful nature with the rest of humanity—so He also deposits the resurrected (incorruptible) seed-life of the Savior within the sinful soul of every believer. The Bible states very clearly that

No one *who abides in Him sins; no one who*

sins has seen Him or knows Him. [7]*Little children, make sure no one deceives you; the one who practices righteousness is righteous, just as He is righteous;* [8]*the one who practices sin is of the devil; for the devil has sinned from the beginning. The Son of God appeared for this purpose, to destroy the works of the devil.* [9]***No one*** *who is born of God practices sin, because* ***His seed abides in him****; and* ***he cannot*** *sin, because* ***he is born of God****.* [10]*By this the children of God and the children of the devil are obvious: anyone who does not practice righteousness is not of God, nor the one who does not love his brother.*

1 John 3:6-9 (Emphasis mine)

The above verses clearly portray the divergent lifestyles of the two classes of people who walk the earth. On the one hand, we have those that are of the devil, born in sin and fashioned in iniquity (Psalm 51:5); on the other, those that are of God, born again in righteousness and true holiness (Ephesians 4:24). Adam sold all his descendants into a life of slavery to sin; Christ came to deliver Adam's children by destroying the works of the evil one (sin) in their lives.

In addition, the Biblical text confirms that all who are

born of God—that is, born again through faith in Jesus Christ—do not live a life of sin, because born-again life contains the incorruptible seed of God which cannot sin. Whenever the believer is centered in, and governed by, this inner seed-life of God, he cannot sin, for **_No one_** who _abides in Him_ sins. . . (1 John 3:6).

Sin is always a product of the Adam man or natural life. It is NEVER the work of the inner spirit-man. Sin is always self-centered—self-preserving or self-benefiting, but NEVER, EVER, is it Christ-centered. This incorruptible seed-life of Christ within the believer is not only sinless, but also sin-proof. The Bible says that **it cannot sin**. The evil one cannot even touch it because it is born of God and the Son of God guards it (1 John 5:18; 1 Peter 1:5). This is the life that is hidden with Christ, in God—all spirit, no flesh (Colossians 3:3).

Through faith in what Christ did, and what God says, the believer must lay hold of the truth that his real life (incorruptible spirit-life) is out of the reach of satan and sin. Whenever the child of God steps out of his secured position in Christ through unbelief, or because of some perceived threat or advantage to his Adam self, he opens the door to satan and sin. This scenario represents the conditional _"if"_ in 1 John 1:8. Apart from that, it is totally unfeasible for that life abiding in Christ to sin, and equally impossible for natural life, centered in Adam, NOT to sin.

This is certainly very contrary to the belief systems of many professing Christianity, who all their lives have tried in vain to serve God through the platform of their Adam soul-life. They misunderstand and misrepresent 1 John 3:9 because they view and interpret this scripture through the filter of their faltering soul (flesh). Many believers still call themselves sinners because they continue to identify themselves by the experiences of their soul-life, while at the same time claiming they are born again of the incorruptible seed of Christ's Spirit.

Sin is always self-centered— self-preserving or self-benefiting, but NEVER, EVER Christ-centered.

How confused and sad a condition in which to live one's experience as a professing follower of Christ! So many of God's children go through life trying to convince others to become Christians, while they, themselves, are living without any genuine assurance of full salvation and deliverance from sin. They keep struggling daily with their failing Adam, hoping to become righteous at the return of Jesus.

Righteousness is a quality of spirit-life (Christ's); NEVER the work of flesh (Adam's). It exists only in the inner Christ-man of the believer's spirit; NEVER in the Adam-man of his fleshly soul. Some will argue, I am sure, that "'we' can NEVER be without sin on this side of eternity." These may even cite 1 John 1:8-10 as supporting Biblical evidence for their position. Well, let's examine these scriptures and see what they really mean.

> *If we say that we have no sin, we deceive ourselves, and the truth is not in us. ⁹If we confess our sins, he is faithful and just to forgive us our sins, and to cleanse us from all unrighteousness. ¹⁰If we say that we have not sinned, we make him a liar, and his word is not in us.*

1 John 1:8-10, KJV

First of all, we must understand the reference to the collective "we" in the apostle John's statement in this text. Is he speaking of the "we" as in the soul-man of our Adam life, or "we" as in the inner spirit-man of our Christ life? I believe that John's reference to the "we" in the above scripture is very similar to that of Paul's "I" and "me" in Romans 7:14-25, when he spoke of his struggles with his sin nature before his life-transforming encounter with Christ.

The "we" of 1 John 1:8-10, and the "I" and "me" of Romans 7, both refer to the self that is driven by the power of the natural or flesh life. This life cannot claim "sinlessness" at any given moment of time, because it was born in sin and fashioned in iniquity (Psalm 51:5). It is, and will always be, sinful. It is only in this context, *if we say that we have no sin, we deceive ourselves, and the truth is not in us . . . ¹⁰If we say that we have not sinned, we make him a liar, and his word is not in us* (1 John 1:8, 10).

However, when the child of God discovers his true identity by focusing his attention on the reality of the Christ-man within him, he is empowered through grace—the union of Christ's Spirit and his—to gain dominion over the power of sin in his soul. This is where the apostle Paul found

Righteousness is a quality of spirit-life; NEVER the work of flesh.

the answer to his fleshly dilemma and cried out: "*I thank God through Jesus Christ our Lord . . .*" (Romans 7:25). Then he immediately went on to say:

> *There is therefore <u>now</u> <u>no condemnation</u> to <u>them which are in Christ Jesus</u>, who walk not after the flesh, but after the Spirit. ²For <u>the law of the Spirit of life</u> <u>in Christ Jesus</u> hath <u>made me free</u> from <u>the law of sin and death</u> [in Adam].*

> Romans 8:1-2, KJV, brackets mine

The believer's life in Christ—not in Adam—is a life in the spirit that enjoys full and complete justification before

God. Therefore, he does not live with the threat of judgment hanging over his head, but conducts his life in freedom as a son of God and joint-heir with Jesus Christ to eternal inheritance in the Father's kingdom (Romans 8:15-17).

The Bible says that the law (or principle) of the Spirit of life in Christ Jesus has made him completely free from the law (or principle) of sin and death that exist in his Adam nature. In other words, this "inner-spirit-directed" believer is no longer driven by the power (or law) of his sinful nature, but by the power of a sinless, indestructible life—Christ Jesus—that indwells his spirit. It is the power of Christ's life, operating within, that makes him absolutely free from the power and consequence of sin.

Christ is not only the solution for our acts of sin, as reflected in 1 John 1:9. He is also the only solution for our life of sin, as reflected in Romans 7. Through His death on the cross, Christ released us completely from the law of sin and death that bound us in marriage to Adam's sinful nature; and by His victorious resurrection, He united us in marriage to Himself and His indestructible, sinless life. This is the truth clearly expressed in Romans 7:1-6 and Colossians 2:11-13 (Please take the time to study these scriptures).

Additionally, it must also be remembered that the John who said, *"if we say that we have no sin, we deceive ourselves, and the truth is not in us"* (1 John 1:8), is also the John who later said that *"those who have been born of God do not sin, because God's seed abides in them; they cannot sin, because they have been born of God*" (1 John 3:9, NRSV).

Is this a contradiction of thought, or some measure of theological confusion on the part of John? Absolutely not! What is born of God is not the fallen, natural man of Adam, but the inner spirit-man of Christ in the believer. This natural man we inherited from Adam will always be sinful, because he was born from a seed of corruption. Absolutely NOTHING can be done to change that reality. The inner spirit-man of our Christ nature will always be sinless, because he was born from incorruptible seed; and absolutely NOTHING can be done to change that reality.

This is what being born again is really all about. It's about the life of God taking up residence in the natural life of fallen man; the kingdom of light entering the kingdom of darkness; victorious spirit invading hopeless flesh. In this reality, incorruption indwells corruption but "should not be" dominated by it. I said "should not be"

> *Christ is not only the solution for our acts of sin. He is also the only solution for our life of sin.*

because the will of the believer is the judge as to who will rule over his house of seeds — spirit or flesh.

However, Christ has already bound the strongman (the devil) who once reigned over the believer's fleshly house, and now seeks the believer's cooperation to spoil the works of the devil within his soul (1 John 3:8; Matthew 12:22-29).

Ultimately then, the child of God must choose daily to live from his real identity in Christ, while denying all that pertains to the fleshly, natural man of his Adam self (Matthew 16:24). This is the distinctive hallmark of victorious Christian living. The born-again believer can only sin whenever he is controlled by his natural life from Adam; but he CANNOT sin whenever he is under the control his spirit life from Christ. It is totally impossible for the Christ-man within his incorruptible seed-life to sin because he is born of God (1 John 3:9).

Daily victories over sin simply become a matter of the believer knowing and implementing his walk by the Spirit, and he will not fulfill the sinful desires of his flesh (Galatians 5:16). How this is done is the discussion of the remaining chapters of this book.

Truth-Nuggets Summary

1. *The born-again spirit-man is a brand new creation from heaven; not an adjustment or improvement of the natural Adam man from earth.*

2. *The born-again spirit-man is a divine creation that is rooted in Christ, the life-giving Spirit.*

3. *Born-again life is not only sinless. It is also sin-proof.*

Notes:

1. For more details on Paul's "in Christ" expression, please read my earlier volume, *Imitating God: The Amazing Secret of Living His Life* (Berrien Springs, Rehoboth Publishing, 2011), 64-70.
2. http://www.todayifoundout.com/index.php/ 2011/10/caterpillars-melt-almost-completely- before-growing-into-butterflies-in-the- chrysalis/#UXr2FrCTWITZE3ZT.99

Let the same mind be in you that was in Christ Jesus.

Philippians 2:5, NRSV

Chapter 5

BORN AGAIN:
RENEWING MY THINKING

The Bible teaches very clearly that there are irreconcilable differences between the mind of the believer's inner spirit-man and that of his natural or soul man. In this reality, the mind of the born-again spirit-man is really and truly the righteous mind of Christ; whereas the mind of the believer's soul-man is really the sinful, corrupt mind of Adam. This is the mind that the Word of God describes as vain, dark and separated from the life of God.

> So I tell you this, and insist on it in the Lord, that you must no longer live as the Gentiles do, *in the futility of their thinking*. [18]They are darkened in their understanding and *separated from the life of God* because of *the ignorance that is in them due to the hardening of their hearts*. [19]Having *lost all sensitivity*, they have given themselves over to sensuality so as to indulge in every kind of impurity, with a continual lust for more.

Ephesians 4:17-19, NIV

This scripture gives a very clear picture of the mind that characterizes every child of Adam. It is a mind that is self-centered and self-driven, running totally on natural intelligence and human reason. It is guided by a reality that is shaped by human perception of reality. Through sin, the spirit of Adam, which was designed for direct communion with God, became alienated from the life of God—the Spirit of light and love (1 John 1:5; 4:8).

This estrangement from God left Adam and his descendants in an inner and outer world of impenetrable darkness. Stripped of the light and wisdom which came through his direct link with his Creator, Adam's heart and mind became the stronghold of the demons of darkness and deception. It is this dreadful legacy of deepening darkness that hangs as a pall of death over the people of this age (Isaiah 60:2), driving Adam's children to all kinds of immoral and lustful excesses, void of shame or any type of remorse (Ephesians 4:19).

God's Mercy

> *For it is the <u>God</u> who said, "Let light shine out of darkness," who <u>has shone in our hearts</u> to give the light of the knowledge of the glory of God in the face of Jesus Christ. [7]But <u>we have this treasure in clay jars</u>, so that it may*

be made clear that this extraordinary power
belongs to God and does not come from us.

Corinthians 4:6-7, NRSV

In His super-abounding mercy, God shone His light of life and love into our darkness when, through His eternal Spirit, He deposited the incorruptible seed of the glorious Light of the world within our hearts. This light is the born-again, spirit-life of Jesus within the believer. Notice that verse 7 of the text says that God's treasured Light of life is within the clay jar of our Adam or soul-man. This truth the child of God must never forget, because it is the only power-source for his life of victory over the world and sin. The mind of the born-again believer is driven by the power of God within his spirit; not the power of human reason arising from his fleshly soul.

Hence, Paul reminded the born-again Ephesians: "*you were formerly darkness, but now you are Light in the Lord; walk as children of Light*" (Ephesians 5:8). In other words, do not live by the dictates of your naturally vain and darkened mind, as do unconverted clay people. Instead, he suggested the following:

> *But you did not <u>learn Christ</u> in this way, ²¹if*
> *indeed you have heard Him and have been*

taught in Him, just as <u>truth is in Jesus</u>, [22]that, in reference to your former manner of life, you lay aside the old self, which is being corrupted in accordance with the lusts of deceit, [23]and that you <u>be renewed</u> in <u>the spirit of your mind</u>, [24]and put on <u>the new self</u>, which <u>in the likeness of God</u> <u>has been created</u> <u>in righteousness and holiness of the truth</u>.

Ephesians 4:20-24

The above text hints that there are really only two ways of thinking available to all humanity—like Adam or like Christ. By default we naturally think like Adam, using reason and our perception of reality. This offers only a self-centered direction to life; one that leads to nowhere but to eternal destruction. Proverbs 16:25 says that *there is a way which seems right to a man, but its end is the way of death.*

However, whenever a person is born-again, he is given the mind of Christ, which affords him the capacity to think like his Savior, by leaning on the wisdom and direction of God: Therefore Jesus answered and was saying to them, *"Truly, truly, I say to you, the Son can do nothing of Himself, unless it is something He sees the Father doing; for whatever the Father does, these things the Son also does in like manner"* (John 5:19). This thinking mode offers a God-centered direction to life; one that operates only by *every word of God* (Matthew 4:4).

Hence, Paul could have instructed the Ephesians that they should be renewed in the spirit of their minds, living by the way they had learned Christ, and had been taught in Him (Ephesians 4:20, 23 above). The spirit that controls the mind of the old Adam-man is the spirit of deception and falsehood (Ephesians 4:18; Jeremiah 17:9); but the spirit that runs the born-again mind of the inner-man is the Spirit of Christ (Romans 8:9, 16).

The true view of reality does not reside in fallen mankind. He is ruled by a spirit of disobedience (Ephesians 2:2-3) and self-conceit that distorts the truth. On the other hand, the Bible confirms that the truth exists only in Jesus and His Word

The true view of reality does not reside in fallen mankind.

(Ephesians 4:21; John 14:6; 17:17). Only the divine mind that is imparted to the believer through the incorruptible seed of his inner spirit-life is capable of apprehending and transmitting truth to the life. Therefore, wisdom counsels:

> *Trust in the LORD with all your heart and <u>do not lean on your own understanding</u>. ⁶In <u>all your ways</u> acknowledge Him, and He will make your paths straight. ⁷<u>Do not be wise in your own eyes</u>; Fear the LORD and turn away*

from evil . . .

Proverbs 3:5-7

Truth-Nugget #1: *The mind of the inner spirit-man thinks and operates independently from, and contrary to, the mind of natural soul-man.*

Opposing Forces

For <u>the flesh</u> sets its desire against <u>the Spirit</u>, and the Spirit against the flesh; for <u>these are in opposition to one another</u>, so that you may not do the things that you please.

Galatians 5:17

The born-again life of the child of God inhabits an earthly tent that has been sold to the devil since the beginning of time. This tent characterizes everything pertaining to natural human existence or "the self," including emotions, thought-life and behavior—altogether referred to as flesh. The kingdom of light in the believer's spirit has invaded the kingdom of darkness of his fleshly soul, waging war against all the works of the devil, causing God's light—the life of Jesus—to shine out of darkness—the believer's fleshly body

(See 2 Corinthians 4:6, 7 above).

The mind of Christ's Spirit within the believer is in constant conflict with his fleshly mind from Adam. These two can never harmonize, because they originate from two opposing natures—one of righteous and un-approachable light (1 Timothy 6:15-16), and the other, of wickedness and impenetrable darkness. They are always in continuous conflict, striving to control the will (or decision-center) of the believer. The spirit of lust arising from the believer's old Adam nature may tempt him/her to steal, lie, cheat or violate some moral code of conduct, but the Spirit of Christ, operating through the voice of conscience will actively contest these carnal desires.

As a young Christian, I remember spending many sleepless moments trying to resolve the battle between my fleshly mind and my Spirit-driven conscience. Every time I tried to find an excuse to commit sin, or to convince myself (really make myself pretend) that my intended plan was okay, my awakened conscience would always stand in the way. The good, but frustrating, thing was, I could not silence or drown the voice of my conscience no matter how hard I tried. Every excuse was met by a clear rebuttal. How many of us have been there, and done that?

I understand now that the mind of my spirit and my natural mind (flesh) operate independently of each other, and, through the action of my will, I can decide which of these two forces will govern the choice I will eventually make. This is the seed of enmity that my loving, heavenly Father planted in me to resist the free flow of satanic evil in my life. All I have to do is to nurture that spirit seed continuously through the witness of the Holy Spirit and the eternal Word of God. Our heavenly Father uses both these instruments—the Word and His Spirit—to renew and reshape our will, weakened by sin, making it more amenable to yield to the influence of the mind of Christ instead of the mind of Adam within us.

Operation Modes

There are very clear distinctions in the modes of operation between the mind of the believer's inner spirit-man and that of his natural man. The apostle Paul addressed this issue quite adequately in his letter to the Christians in Corinth:

> For who among men knows the thoughts of a man except *the spirit of the man* which is in him? Even so *the thoughts of God* no one knows except the Spirit of God. [12]Now we have received, not *the spirit of the world*, but *the Spirit who is from God*, so that we may know the things freely given to us by God,

¹³which things <u>we</u> also <u>speak</u>, <u>not in words</u> <u>taught by human wisdom, but in those taught</u> <u>by the Spirit</u>, combining <u>spiritual thoughts</u> <u>with spiritual words</u>. ¹⁴But <u>a natural man does</u> <u>not accept the things of the Spirit of God</u>, for they are foolishness to him; and <u>he cannot</u> <u>understand them</u>, because <u>they are spiritually</u> <u>appraised</u>. ¹⁵But <u>he who is spiritual appraises</u> <u>all things</u>, yet he himself is appraised by no one.

1 Corinthians 2:11-15

There appear to be five elements arising from the above scripture that indicate distinct levels of operations between the mind of the natural man and that of the born-again spirit-man.

1. *<u>Level of perception (2:11)</u>*. The fleshly mind of the natural-born individual can perceive and understand only thought and ideas about things pertaining to the natural realm. The mind of the person born again by the Spirit can perceive and apprehend the thoughts of God, in a dimension unknown to the children of Adam. This is a total Spirit to spirit (Romans 8:16) transmission, as

Deep communicates with deep (Psalm 42:7).

2. *Level of motivation (2:12)*. The mind of the natural-born man is motivated by the spirit of the world, which is a spirit of pride, lust and disobedience that drives him to live in rebellion against God (1 John 2:15-17; Ephesians 2:2; James 4:4). The mind of the born-again believer is motivated by the Spirit of God that drives him to live in obedience to God.

3. *Level of function (2:13)*. The mind of the un-regenerated person functions on the basis of human logic, comparing natural perception and the human experience with human reason. On the other hand, the mind of the spirit-man functions by combining thoughts and impression, received from the Holy Spirit, with the Spirit Word of God.

4. *Level of receptivity (2:14)*. The natural mind cannot receive the things of the Spirit of God because it is controlled by the powers of the darkness. Spiritual things appear foolish to the natural-born individual because they exist and operate outside the realm of human logic. Only the person born again of the Spirit is capable of accepting and relating to them.

5. *Level of appraisal (2:15)*. This is a follow-through of verse 14. The carnal (natural-born) man can

only evaluate things pertaining to the natural or earthly realm; but the one who is spiritual (born again of the Spirit) is able to evaluate all things—of natural and spiritual origin.

The Mind of Christ

For WHO HAS KNOWN THE MIND OF THE LORD, THAT HE WILL INSTRUCT HIM? But we have the mind of Christ.

1 Corinthians 2:16

In verse 11 of 1 Corinthians 2, Paul introduced the question, *"for who among men knows the thoughts of a man except the spirit of the man which is in him?"* In the last verse of the chapter (2:16), however, he concluded with the ultimate question, *"for WHO HAS KNOWN THE MIND OF THE LORD, THAT HE WILL INSTRUCT HIM?"* Sandwiched between these two questions he showed the divergent operations between the mind of the natural man and the mind of the inner spirit-man.

In the end, he came away with the unalterable truth that born-again believers possess the mind of Christ. This is so because the incorruptible seed-life within all believers is, in truth and in fact, the very life of Jesus. Hence, Paul could have claimed very confidently, *"it is no longer I who live, but Christ lives in me . . ."* (Galatians 2:20). The very sad fact is that many born-again children of God live with a spiritual/mental disconnect because they are out of touch with the reality of Christ's life within their inner spirit-man. Therefore, they operate predominantly, if not totally, from the mind of Adam. These do not really believe that they already have the mind of Christ.

Adding to the dismay is the powerlessness that characterizes the religious experience of these unwary children of God. The Bible confirms that as a man thinks in his heart, so is he (Proverbs 23:7), and out from his heart flows the wellspring of his life (Proverbs 4:23). Thinking like Adam attracts all the negative forces that work against human life. Thinking like Christ produces the power and authority capable of overcoming all the hosts of evil and adversity on the planet, for greater is He who is in us than anything/anyone in the world (1 John 4:4).

Born-again believers possess the mind of Christ.

Hence, the Word of God admonishes us: *Let this mind be in you, which was also in Christ Jesus* (Philippians 2:5, KJV). Notice the text did not say we should try to possess the mind (thinking, attitude, etc.) of Christ. No! On the contrary, the text assumes the presence of the mind of Christ in the believer, and is calling the believer to recognize and surrender to it. Just let it (the mind of Christ) be! Do not fight it! Nurture it! Support it! This calls for putting my way of thinking aside, so that what Christ thinks—as reflected through the Spirit and the Word—becomes the catalyst for my words and actions.

Tapping In

The gnawing question that may be swirling around in your mind right now is how does one tap into the mind of Christ within oneself without confusing its thoughts and ideas with those of one's natural mind? The infallible Word of God is the sole judge over of what originates from the mind of Christ (spirit), and what comes from the mind of Adam (soul). Here is what divine inspiration says:

> For the word of God is _living_ and _active_ and _sharper than any two-edged sword_, and piercing as far as _the division_ of _soul_ and _spirit_, of both joints and marrow, and _able to judge the thoughts and intentions of the heart_.

Hebrews 4:12

The Word of God alone possesses the power to clearly discern and separate what is arising from a person's spirit from that which originates from his soul or natural mind. –

Consequently, if the believer is not outfitted with a working knowledge of the Word of God, he will be quite vulnerable to all forms of satanic deceptions, via physical manifestations, and/or mental and emotional confusion. Quite often one would come across believers who would say that the Spirit told them "thus and so." When they are asked how do they know this for certain, the response often given is, "well, I feel it deep within my spirit."

The human mind, no matter how brilliant, is inherently flawed and totally incapable of sitting as judge over its thoughts and intentions.

However, feeling is not the divine instrument for testing and validating truth. Only the Word of God is. *Thy Word is truth* (John 17:17). Every thought, feeling, hunch or intuitive idea must fall under its strict, impeccable scrutiny. The Bible says that we must test every spirit to see if it is of God — or rather, originates from the mind of Christ — for there are many false prophets (preachers and teachers) in the world who are operating under the influence of lying spirits.

The Word of God is the only divine instrument for testing and validating truth.

> *Beloved, do not believe every spirit, but test the spirits to see whether they are from God, because many false prophets have gone out*

112

into the world.

1 John 4:1

Let the mind of Christ reign in you (Philippians 2:5). That mind is one that is governed only by every word that proceeds from the mouth of God (Matthew 4:4).

Once for All Time

Truth-Nugget #2: *Being born again of the Spirit is a one-time experience, just like being born of the flesh can occur only once.*

Many Christians who misunderstand what it means to be born again often equate it with being baptized. On account of this, many who have strayed away from the faith often seek re-baptism as a means to be born again *again*, to start over *again* a new life in Christ. I have met individuals who have been baptized several times in their efforts to attain what they envision as a true born-again experience. Many who have been overcome by their failure to achieve this goal have either walked away from Christianity altogether, while others are still hoping to find the "right" church or spiritual leader that could make it happen for them.

While baptism is the necessary follow-through and

outward testament that marks the "official" launching of the believer's walk with Christ, it neither initiates the born-again experience nor even confirms it. As a matter of fact, some individuals are baptized for many other mundane reasons than to celebrate new life in Jesus. However, contrary to popular belief, baptism does not and cannot renew an individual, or infuse him with power to live the born-again life.

Baptism does not and cannot renew an individual, or infuse him with power to live the born-again life.

Biblically speaking, baptism brings the reality of Christ's crucifixion, burial and resurrection to bear symbolic witness to the death and burial of the believer's past life of sin, and his resurrection to born-again life in Jesus. Through faith, the believer experiences Calvary and embraces the victorious, resurrected life of Jesus.

> *Or <u>do you not know</u> that all of us who have been baptized into Christ Jesus have been baptized into His death? ⁴Therefore we have been <u>buried with Him</u> through baptism into death, so that as Christ was raised from the dead through the glory of the Father, so we too might walk in newness of life. ⁵For if we have become <u>united with Him</u> in the likeness of His death, certainly we shall also be in the likeness*

of His resurrection, ⁶knowing this, that <u>our old self was crucified with Him</u>, in order that our body of sin might be done away with, so that we would <u>no longer</u> be <u>slaves</u> to sin.

Romans 6:3-6

Interestingly, the Bible goes on to say that once resurrected, Christ will never die again; for He tasted death once for all mankind.

Now if we have died with Christ, we believe that we shall also live with Him, ⁹knowing that Christ, having been raised from the dead, <u>is never to die again</u>; death no longer is master over Him. ¹⁰For the death that He died, He died to sin once for all; but the life that He lives, He lives to God.

Romans 6:8-10

Consequently, since the believer's baptism has a direct correlation to the crucifixion of Jesus Christ, and the Savior will never die again, then multiple baptisms of any believer do not have any real spiritual value whatsoever. They may offer false hope, but never real experience.

Re-baptism does not change or rearrange what God has already done in the spirit of the believer through His grace. The problem with those who use baptism to fix the failings of professed believers is that they have not taught these children of God how to identify and work with born-again spirit-life. Consequently, they target their efforts on the wrong man—the one the believer beholds in the mirror—while inadvertently neglecting the incorruptible inner man of the believer's spirit-life.

> *Re-baptism does not change or rearrange what God has already done in the spirit of the believer through His grace.*

God's Answer to Transgression and Failure

Because identity confusion prevails in all Christian circles, the devil is having a field day with unwary believers. Many Christians get stuck in their Adam self, because that's the identity they see and know so well. However, their spirit identity in Christ is one they cannot see (but must embrace by faith), and one of which they are either totally ignorant or only just beginning to know.

Therefore, the most pressing need of failing Christians is not re-baptism of their Adam life, but a genuine introduction to, and working relationship with, their incorruptible spirit-life in Christ. They need to identify, engage and nurture that life as the true reality of their total experience in Christ. It is God's ONE-TIME gift to all who believe in Jesus Christ. This is not an affirmation of the once saved, always saved doctrine; but it is the very critical issue of a person possessing, but never really having tasted of the *heavenly gift* of God's life within himself.

> For *it is impossible* for those who were *once enlightened*, and have *tasted of the heavenly gift*, and were made partakers of the Holy Ghost, *5And have *tasted the good word of God*, and *the powers of the world to come*, *6If they shall fall away, *to renew them again* unto repentance; seeing they crucify to themselves the Son of God afresh, and put him to an open shame.

> Hebrews 6:4-6

So many who are currently walking in the Christian way have never really experience the reality and power of the heavenly gift of God's life in their spirit. They have lived all their lives trying to please God through the efforts of their fleshly soul, completely oblivious of their true spirit identity in Christ, and of the present reality of the power of the world to come. This sad condition exists, in part or in whole, because of over-exposure to the doctrines of men instead of *the good word of God*—the true gospel of God's love and grace in the gift of Jesus Christ. Authentic, born-again living still remains an elusive fantasy for countless believers, and regarded as an utter impossibility to many others who, for all practical purposes, have given up on "the Way".

However, the truth of the above scripture remains. Once renewed or regenerated by the Holy Spirit, born-again spirit-life cannot be regenerated again and again. The Holy Spirit does not take born-again spirit-life away and give it again a second, third or even fourth time around through the process of re-baptism.

Despite the failings of a person's fleshly Adam, he cannot be born-again *again* of the Holy Spirit. Moreover, fleshly failings do not cancel his standing with God, nor places him out of fellowship with Christ. He remains a child of God; just as my daughters remain my children in spite of their short-comings. I do not believe, for one moment, that erring parents could ever be more gracious to their fleshly children than our heavenly Father is to His spirit children (Matthew 7:11; Hebrew 12:9)

The spirit union that the believer shares with Christ and the Father cannot be broken by sinful missteps. The grace of God is always greater than his sins, and offers him hope to keep on seeking for greater spiritual nourishment. It is the work of the evil one to make the child of God doubt his

Father's grace, so that he would be overcome by hopelessness and fear with regards to his sins and his Father's acceptance. Consequently, he gives up on grace and on himself, and continues to sin all the more. Where most professed Christian communities fail this victim of the enemy is in their choosing the much easier course that executes swift judgment against him, instead of using the spirit of grace and compassion to lift, teach and restore him.

Fleshly failings do not cancel a believer standing with God, nor places him out of fellowship with Christ.

Grace is God's answer for ALL sin, no matter how grave. It is grace, not law, that teaches us how *to live soberly, righteous, and godly in this present world* (Titus 2:12). It is grace that leads to repentance and gets one out of sin's debacle. This grace, contrary to popular belief, is more than just divine favor. It is really the spirit of Jesus operating both in and on behalf of believer. The Bible says that *Christ is full of grace and truth*—really, He is both grace and truth—and *of His fullness we have all received, and grace upon grace* (John 1:14, 16).

The Scriptures further explain that *the Law*, which brings condemnation to the offender, *was given through Moses; but grace and truth came through Jesus Christ* (John 1:17). However, Grace (Jesus) came, not to destroy the Law, but to satisfy or fulfill its righteous demand through a sinless life

Grace is God's answer for ALL sin, no matter how grave.

and a vicarious death (Matthew 5:17). Through faith in God's Grace—really, Jesus Christ—the believer is completely justified or accepted by God. *For God [He] hath made Him to be sin for us, who knew no sin; that we might become the righteousness of God in Him* (2 Corinthians 5:21).

Contrary to the logic of popular opinion that Law acts as a deterrent to sin, the Bible says that *the strength of sin is the Law* (1 Corinthian 15:56). *The Law came in so that transgression might increase; but where sin increased, grace abounded all the more* (Romans 5:20). The truth is, the more laws you add to any human system, the more sin and corruption will pervade in that system. For instance, whenever new rules are added to a game of sports, more violations are committed, and more players receive penalties. There are just so many more rules/laws for players to violate.

Law invokes all types of sinful lust in human nature (Romans 7:8), and prohibitions have a tendency to provoke curiosity, inquiry and impulsivity. A person walks into a freshly painted room and sees a sign that says, "Wet paint. Do not touch." Instinctively, the person is provoked to touch the wall, may be just to see if the wall was still wet. The funny thing is, if there was no sign near the wall, that same individual may just go about his/her business without even noticing the wall.

It is just simply amazing, even frustrating at times, to see how telling a person not to do something, unfolds into the very thing you told him not to do. People will see signs saying: "Switch off your cell-phone when approaching the teller," and they will just keep their conversations going. "Don't text while driving," and they will just keep right on texting. What is it about laws and rules that invoke people to break them? It is

The more laws you add to any human system, the more sin and corruption will pervade in that system.

sin—the spirit of demonic disobedience and rebellion—which resides in the human nature (Ephesians 2:2).

Thankfully, God's answer to more sin is more grace (Jesus), not more law; for where sin abounds, grace super-abounds (Romans 5:20). Some religious people are very uncomfortable about more grace for sinners—but not for themselves, obviously. These fear that more grace will provide sinners an excuse for sin. They fail to see that Grace (Jesus) is the sinner's ONLY hope and SINGLE source of empowerment to resist and overcome sin. Moreover, they often forget that their own standing before God is ALWAYS totally one of grace, and NEVER one of any human merit. They continuously receive what ALL sinners need and can never be worthy of. That's why it—rather, He—is called Grace; because NO ONE really deserves Him.

IT IS SIN, NOT SELF-RIGHTEOUSNESS, WHICH ATTRACTS GOD'S GRACE. God has shut up ALL humanity—the self-righteous and the un-righteous—in sin and disobedience so that He could shower His grace and mercy upon ALL (Romans 11:32). For God so loved the world [of sinner] that He gave His ONLY grace package— Jesus Christ—to redeem ALL who believe in Him (John 3:16). Grace (Jesus) once told the self-righteous, judgmental Pharisees: *"It is not those who are healthy who need a physician, but those who are sick But go and learn what this means: 'I DESIRE COMPASSION, AND NOT SACRIFICE,' for I did not come to call the righteous, but sinners"* (Matthew 9:12-13).

Consequently, our response to a believer's missteps should not be one of judgment, but one of graceful restoration. God did not call us to be law-enforcement agents, but ambassadors of grace, reconciling humanity to Him (2 Corinthians 5:18-20). When a believer is overtaken by sin, what he needs more than ever is not condemnation, followed by re-baptism. What we need is compassion and spiritual empowerment. The brother/sister should be instructed and supported in learning how to walk consistently by the Spirit and the Word, so that his/her life would be one of sustained victory over fleshly corruption (Galatians 5:16).

IT IS SIN, NOT SELF-RIGHTEOUSNESS, WHICH ATTRACTS GOD'S GRACE.

However, once that person has connected with, and tasted of, the true life of God and the powers of eternal life within himself, being lost is an utter impossibility unless and until he deliberately chooses to deny and/or reject that life for a life of open rebellion against his Maker. But as long as he is actively seeking after God, his spirit will never be separated from the Spirit and life of His Savior.

> *For if we go on sinning willfully after receiving the knowledge of the truth, there no longer remains a sacrifice for sins, ²⁷but a terrifying expectation of judgment and THE FURY OF A FIRE WHICH WILL CONSUME THE ADVERSARIES. ²⁸Anyone who has set aside the Law of Moses dies without mercy on the testimony of two or three witnesses. ²⁹How much severer punishment do you think he will deserve who has trampled under foot the Son of God, and has regarded as unclean the blood of the covenant by which he was sanctified, and has insulted the Spirit of grace?*

Hebrews 10:26-29

It is very important to know that the only thing that can cancel the born-again spirit-life of the believer is his WILLFUL, DELIBERATE choice to live a life of sin and revolt against God. Such a decision will invalidate the

The only thing that could cancel the born-again spirit-life of the believer is his WILLFUL, DELIBERATE, choice to live a life of sin and revolt against God.

sacrifice of Christ and the ministry of the Holy Spirit on his behalf. The Bible indicates very clearly that the person making such a choice has, in reality, *trampled underfoot the Son of God, regarded as unclean the blood of the covenant by which he was sanctified, and has insulted the Spirit of grace* (Hebrews 10:29).

However, we must also quickly note from the above scripture that Christ will not die again to release incorruptible, resurrected life to any individual, if he recognizes and willfully denies the life he had already received. In other words, there will not be a born-again repeat, for the Holy Spirit will not regenerate new life in that individual. Sadly, he will be an eternally lost soul. I sincerely pray that this will never be the experience of any reader of this volume.

It is Personal

Truth Nugget #3:

Born-again means living totally and completely by the reality of Christ's life within my spirit; not Adam's life within my soul.

Born-again living is a total faith experience in which I receive as my very own, all that Christ did, all that He offers and all that He represents on my behalf. Christ and I share the same spirit (1 Corinthians 6:17) and His life is mine forever (Colossians 3:3, 4). *Born-again* means living by what God's says about me in His Word, and not by what I or others think or feel about me. I live by my identity in Christ, not by my identity in Adam.

Christ and I share the same spirit, and His life is mine forever.

The real me is a spirit being from heaven, the true country of my citizenship (Philippians 3:20). I must confess and live this reality every moment of every day until it becomes my first nature, totally replacing the old nature I once shared with Adam. It is *the law of the Spirit of life in Christ Jesus that has set me free [completely] from the law of sin and death*, which was Adam's legacy to me (Roman 8:2, bracket mine).

Christ's Example

Although Christ walked the earth in a human body for a mere thirty-three or so years, He repeatedly told His followers and His accusers that He was from heaven. He saw Joseph and Mary only as His surrogate parents (Luke 2:40-50; Mark 3:32-35), but consistently referred to God Almighty as His true Father (John 8:18-19, 28-29, 42; 16:26-28). "*I and the Father are one*"

125

(John 10:30) transcended all the earthly associations of Jesus. In other words, Jesus completely identified Himself by, and always gave precedence to, His everlasting life from above; not His very brief existence from below.

While through His body Christ established connection with the sinful human race, through His Spirit life from above, He completely identified and maintained union with the righteous life of God. This is the example He has left for us, His brethren (Hebrews 2:11). If we are to live victoriously as born-again believers who bear the very image of Christ in our spirits, we must follow in the footsteps of our Savior. We must identify ourselves completely by our life from Christ above, not by the fleeting shadow (Job 14:1, 2) we received from Adam below.

God's view of the reality of our existence is that we have died—through the crucifixion of Christ on the cross (Galatians 2:20; Romans 6:3-9)—and our true lives are hidden with Christ in Him (Colossians 3:3). Therefore, we are admonished in God's Word to fix our focus on the things that pertain to our life from above, and not on the things that characterize our fleeting existence on earth.

Jesus once made this very profound statement to His disciples, and, I daresay, to all those who would believe in Him through the disciples' witness (John 17:20): "*In that day you will know that I am in My Father, and you in Me, and I in you*" (John 14:20). This is the ultimate experience awaiting every born-again believer—to see himself in God, and God in himself.

Whenever that day occurs for you, then you will come to the revelation that the Father, Christ and you are one, and that your divine identity transcends all other earthly views of yourself and all the other relationships in your life. May "*that day*" for you be TODAY!

Truth Nuggets Summary

1. *The mind of the inner spirit-man thinks and operates independently from the mind of natural soul-man.*

2. *Being born again of the Spirit is a one-time experience, just like being born of the flesh can occur only once.*

3. *Born-again means living totally and completely by the reality of Christ's life within my spirit, not Adam's life within my soul.*

For we are God's workmanship, created in Christ Jesus to do good works, which God prepared in advance for us to do.

Ephesians 2:10, NIV

Chapter 6

BORN AGAIN:
LIVING CHRIST'S LIFE

*"I <u>have been</u> crucified with Christ; and <u>it is
no longer I who live</u>, <u>but it is Christ</u> who lives
in me; and <u>the life I now live in the flesh I live
by faith in the Son of God</u>, who loved me and
gave Himself for me."*

Galatians 2:20, NRSV

The goal of this chapter is to share how the reality and power of Christ's spirit within the believer shape and direct his daily thoughts and life. In order to accomplish this, we will integrate the three indispensable elements of the born-life of Jesus that must characterize the daily experience of the believer—namely, identity recognition, identity acceptance, and identity practice. The first two elements were covered in the earlier chapters of this volume, but a brief review is necessary as we incorporate them with the ultimate element of living practice.

Identity Recognition

Truth Nugget #1: *If I do not recognize, understand and live by my true identity in Christ, I can never gain dominion over satan and sin.*

> "*I have been crucified . . . I no longer live . . . it is Christ who lives . . .*"

Galatians 2:20, NIV

The primary and most important element to living the born-again Christ-life is the believer's knowledge of his identity in Christ and his ability to separate it from that which he "once" possessed in Adam. This is a major issue because it exerts the most powerful influence on the outcome of the born-again experience. The believer cannot live, with any degree of success, an identity which he possesses but is totally unable to recognize. Without such recognition, he can never gain dominion over satan and sin.

More than any other Biblical figure, God inspired the apostle Paul to share extensively on this very critical matter. Through the above scripture, the apostle made a very concise, clear statement regarding the believer's identity in Christ and its relation to the one he once shared with Adam. He said: "*I have been crucified with Christ; and it is no longer I who* _live, but it is Christ_ who lives in me . . ." (Galatians 2:20).

Through faith in Christ's sacrifice on Calvary, the born-again believer must treat as dead the life that once identified him with his Adam nature. But how does one do this? Paul said that we must _consider ourselves [yourselves] to be dead to sin, but alive to God in Christ Jesus_ (Romans 6:11). _Consider_ means to settle it in your mind. This requires an act of the human will and confession of the lips (Romans 10:8-11). An individual must first believe—God—that he is, indeed, dead to sin in Jesus Christ before this act of faith receives the infusion of God's power to keep dead what the Almighty has declared dead. Here is another nugget from Paul:

> . . . _[13]No longer present your members to sin as instruments of wickedness, but present yourselves to God as those who have been brought from death to life, and present your members to God as instruments of righteousness . . . [19]For just as you once presented your members as slaves to impurity and to greater and greater iniquity, so now present your members as slaves to righteousness for sanctification._

> Romans 6:13, 19, NRSV

The word, *present*, in the above scripture suggests the element of choice available to the believer, through the empowerment of God's grace (verse 12) in his spirit and the act of his will. Incorruptible, born-again life within the believer gives him the ability either to present (surrender) the members of his body as servants of righteousness, or to withhold them from being used as instruments of sin.

In Colossians 3:5, Paul was more straightforward in his instruction when he wrote: "*Put to death, therefore, whatever belongs to your earthly nature: sexual immorality, impurity, lust, evil desires and greed, which is idolatry*" (Colossians 3:5). How does one accomplish this? Simple! Stop feeding sin's lusts! Every act of sin is the result of feeding sin's lusts. James wrote: "*But each one is tempted when he is carried away and enticed by his own lust. [15]Then when lust has conceived, it gives birth to sin; and when sin is accomplished, it brings forth death*" (James 1:14-15).

Law of Life

There is a simple law of life that says *whatever we do not feed will die!* This is certainly the case with sin's lust. Paul's admonition is that believers put to death all that belong to our sinful nature (Colossians 3:5). In other words, we are to agree and confirm what

> *Every act of sin is the result of feeding sin's lusts.*

God did through Calvary by starving the diverse lusts of our old nature. Quit feeding sin's lusts! *We feed through what we allow our mind to receive and focus upon*. Our moral or amoral diet reinforces two competing mind-sets—spirit and flesh—that hold sway over ALL the actions of our lives. The Bible says,

> *For those who are according to the flesh <u>set their minds on the things of the flesh</u>, but those who are according to the Spirit, <u>the things of the Spirit</u> . . . [7]because <u>the mind set on the flesh is hostile toward God</u>; for it does not subject itself to the law of God, for it is not even able to do so, [8]and <u>those who are in the flesh cannot please God</u>.*

> Romans 8:5-8

Through the portals of our five senses, especially our sight and hearing, we stimulate, strengthen and impregnate fleshly lusts that war against the inner-man of our spirit. Where we feed, and that on which we feed, will either strengthen God's life in our spirit or resurrect to life what God put to death through Christ on Calvary's cross. Through the power of choice, the believer has equal access to both. How he identifies himself will influence the feeding source he chooses and also his feeding pattern; and both of these will determine whether his acts are acts of sin or of righteousness.

However, the truth remains for those who believe—that is, when Christ died, we died. He did not only die for us, but most importantly, He died *as* us. We were crucified when he was crucified. The apostle Paul further explains this truth in the following way:

> . . . *having concluded this, that <u>one died for all, therefore all died</u>; [15]and He died for all, so that <u>they who live might no longer live for themselves</u>, <u>but for Him who died and rose again on their behalf</u>.*

Corinthians 5:14-15

It is a settled matter in heaven that in the death of Christ all humanity died, whether they choose to believe it or not. That's God's gracious redemptive provision for all. Those who, through faith in God's Gift, embrace the reality of this truth have the privilege of experiencing the power of the resurrected life of Jesus. The Bible states very clearly that these dear children of God no longer live for themselves—that is, by the dictates of

It is a settled matter in heaven that in the death of Christ all humanity died, whether they choose to believe it or not.

reason associated with their natural life—but for the One (Jesus) who died and rose again for them.

Identity Acceptance

Truth-Nugget #2: *The born-again person must accept his union with Christ and his heavenly origin as the realities through which he views and interacts with the world.*

Christ is my [our] life . . .

Colossians 3:4

The resurrected Christ is the believer's new identity. The Bible says that if we have been planted together (through baptism by immersion) in the likeness of His death, we shall be raised (in newness of "born-again" life) in the likeness of His resurrection (Romans 6:5; Colossians 2:12). When Christ died on the cross, He was "planted" in the earth in the body of Adam. When He rose from the dead, He came forth as the eternal life-giving Spirit, clothed in a celestial house—the one made without hands, reserved in heaven for the righteous until His return for them (1 Corinthians 15:42-49; 2 Corinthians 5:1-5).

Consequently, while born-again believers await their incorruptible celestial bodies at the return of Jesus, their incorruptible, inner spirit-man lives and groans in a house of corruption—the body of Adam (2 Corinthians 5:1-4). Paul reminds us that *our citizenship is in heaven, and it is from there that we are expecting a Savior, the Lord Jesus Christ.* *[21]He will transform the body of our humiliation that it may be conformed to the body of his glory, by the power that also enables him to make all things subject to himself*' (Philippians 3:20, NRSV). In Romans, he says:

> *and not only the creation, but we ourselves, who have the first fruits of the Spirit, <u>groan inwardly</u> while we wait for adoption, <u>the redemption of our bodies</u>.*

> Romans 8:23, NRSV

The incorruptible seed of our inner spirit-man is not at home in our body of sin and death, and, therefore, longs for redemption and release. However, while we wait, we must not allow ourselves to be distracted by our old Adam man and lose sight of who we really are in Christ. Paul admonishes that we should cease to recognize or identify ourselves by our fleshly characteristics, and embrace our spirit-unity with Christ (2 Corinthians 5:16; 1 Corinthians 6:17). We must hold to the truth that every law of our human nature that once bound us in marriage to Adam has been annulled by death, so that we could be free to marry another—that is Christ (Romans 7:1-4).

Therefore, as believers, we have a completely new divine identity. That identity is in Christ, not Adam. WE MUST ACCEPT AND BELIEVE THIS! God created us anew in Christ (Ephesians 2:10). Colossian 3:4 says very clearly that Christ is our life, and that we should live by faith (or confidence) in that life, not in ourselves (Galatians 2:20). That's the life that has already conquered satan, sin and the world (John 16:33), and that has every spiritual blessing we need for abundant life and godliness (Ephesians 1:3; 2 Peter 1:3).

Not of Earth

Therefore if you have been raised up with Christ, keep seeking the things above, where Christ is, seated at the right hand of God. ²Set your mind on the things above, not on the things that are on earth.

Colossians 3:1-2

The Bible says very clearly that if *we [you] have been raised up* from the dead *with Christ*—and indeed we have (Romans 6:3-5; Ephesians 2:4-6)—*keep seeking the things above*. We are to *set our [your] mind on the things above, not on things that are on earth* (Colossians 3:1-2). Why are we given these instructions? I believe that among the possible reasons, two are very prominent—namely, so that (1) we can recognize our new identity, and (2), we can embrace and preserve that identity by pursuing the things associated with it.

When Christ died, everything associated with His human life—the embodiment of ALL our sins—died with Him, and so did everything associated with our life. However, when He rose from the dead, He came forth with everything associated

Our real life is not from earth, but from heaven.

with His life from above, and this is the essence our identity in Him. Our real life is not from earth, but from heaven; but how many Christians really believe and live that way? Even before He went to the cross, the Savior repeatedly illustrated that born-again believers are not from this world, but from heaven.

> "*If you were of the world, the world would love its own; but because <u>you are not of the world</u>, but I chose you out of the world, because of this the world hates you.*"

John 15:19

"I have given them Your word; and the world has hated them, because <u>they are not of the world</u>, even as <u>I am not of the world</u>."

John 17:14

"<u>They are not of the world</u>, even as <u>I am not of the world</u>."

John 17:16

Why is it that so many professed Christians are living in contradiction of this truth? Why do so many go out of their way for the world to love and honor them? Is it because they do not really understand the truth about their identity, or because they do not believe Jesus? Could it be that they simply choose to ignore their authentic identity for some perceived fleshly advantage in this world? The Bible says that the world does not really know the real children of God (1 John 3:1), yet so many who profess that name often weary themselves chasing after worldly attention. How strange indeed!

Where are you, dear reader, on this very important identity issue? How do you really view yourself? I believe the best way to find out is to check your "things focus." According to the Word of God, your "things focus" is a true reflection of your understanding of your real identity.

Children from above focus their attention on the things from above, and those from earth, on the things that pertain to this world. Paul also validated this truth in Roman 8:5 when he wrote:

> *For those who live according to the flesh <u>set their minds on</u> the things of the flesh, but those who live according to the Spirit <u>set their minds on</u> the things of the Spirit.*

Romans 8:5, NRSV

How does one determine his "things focus"? Well, here are a couple of questions that can help bring some clarity to this matter. (1) *What is the real driving force of your life?* Is it the love of Christ, or the love of this world? (2) *What's your real reason for living?* Is it to glorify God, or to have enough to live comfortably in this world? (3) *Where do you find your greatest joy, and exert your best energies?* Is it in the pursuit of the things pertaining to this world, or those concerning the kingdom of God? (4) *How would you truly describe your life?* Would you say it is one of peace and sweet rest, or one filled with anxiety and worry over your future?

Your "things" focus is a true reflection of your understanding of your real identity.

- If your answers are (1) the love of Christ; (2) glorifying God; (3) things concerning the kingdom of God; and (4) peace and sweet rest; then you are reflecting characteristics of the identity associated with Spirit of Christ and His kingdom—that is, the "things-from-above" focus.

- On the other hand, if your answers are the other four alternatives, then you are reflecting an identity associated with mind of Adam and the spirit of this world, characterized by anxiety over the things of this life (Matthew 6:25-32)—that is, the "things-from-below" focus.

- Further, if your answers are a mixture of the two previous categories of responses, then you are reflecting, to some degree, the symptom of identity confusion. You are a victim of the **"caterpillar effect"**. In other words, you are thinking like a caterpillar while hoping you could take to the air like a butterfly.

People who suffer from the **"caterpillar effect"** try, unsuccessfully, to serve God through their identity in Adam; but the truth is that those who operate from this fleshly platform plainly cannot please God (Romans 8:5-8). "CATERPILLARS"

The flesh-and-blood individual, born of a woman, CANNOT live the life of Christ—he just cannot fly.

SIMPLY CANNOT FLY! They are not internally and aerodynamically designed for flying. ONLY butterflies (born-again caterpillars, if you may) are designed this way and can fly. Similarly, the flesh-and-blood individual, born of a woman, CANNOT live the life of Christ—he just cannot fly. ONLY the spirit-man, born-again of God with LIFE from above, CAN!

Victims of the **"caterpillar effect"** fail to conceive and accept themselves as **"christ"** (with a lowercase C— i.e. the life of Christ within), and, therefore, take their directions from their everyday experiences in their Adam state. Christ is often related to as a person in the distant heavens, not as the incorruptible seed of his spirit-life within the soul.

However, the Bible says that as He (Christ) is, so are we in this world (1 John 4:17). We are commissioned by God, Himself, to operate in the Savior's place (2 Corinthians 5:20). Until we recognize and accept **"christ"** as our true, born-again identity, we will never experience the joy of the **"butterfly effect"**—that of taking to the air and sampling the sweet "nectar" of God's super-abundant provision and blessings.

Identity Practice

". . . the life I now live . . . I live by faith

in the Son of God . . ."

– Galatians 2:20

The believer's ability to live like Christ is not a matter of his controlling his attitude and behavior, as it is the matter of his believing and assuming his identity within, and focusing daily on his Model for living that identity—Jesus Christ. The issue is one of *faith* and *focus*, and not one of behavior modification.

Faith

Truth Nuggets #3: *Who and what we believe will direct the course of our life.*

Do I really believe that I am who God says I am—a son and not a slave (John 1:12; Romans 8:15-16)? Do I really believe that God did what He said He did through Jesus Christ for me, and *as* me—i.e. in my place (2 Corinthians 5:14; Hebrews 2:9; Galatians 2:20)? Do I really believe that I have the righteous life of Jesus within my spirit (Colossians 3:3-4, 10)? Do I really believe that I was born-again righteous, or do I regard myself a sinner hoping to become righteous one of these days (1 Peter 1:23; 2 Corinthians 5:21; Ephesians 4:24)? Do I believe that I am a born-again spirit being, or am I just a changed human being trying to be spiritual (John 3:6; 1:12-13; 4:24 – God is Spirit, and the Father of spirits—Hebrews 12:9)? What's the real condition of my faith (Hebrews 11:6; 1 John 5:4)? Essentially, the ultimate question really is, "Do I really believe God, or do I believe 'me' more than God?" "Do I really trust God, or do I trust 'me' more than God?"

The truthful answers to all these questions—based on the Word, not merely on one's opinion about oneself— lie at the very foundation of the journey towards authentic Christ-like living. The believer must begin here or he will be on a collision course with frustration and failure as far as imitating Christ is concerned. These are the very questions that I have attempted to answer in the first five chapters of this little book. I sincerely hope you did not miss them. If you did, re-read the chapters while reviewing the scriptures in the parentheses above.

The Most Important Work

The most important "work" designed for living the Christ' life is the "work" of believing God and the Messiah who came from Him. Jesus once had this conversation with an inquiring Jewish crowd who posed the following question to Him: "*What shall we do, that we may work the works of God?*" The answer Christ gave was very interesting and also quite pertinent to our conversation in this book.

> *"This is the work of God, that you believe in Him whom He has sent."*

John 6:29

It is very important to notice that the Jews inquired about doing *the works of God* (plural); but Jesus answered them with a singular noun, "This is *the work of God*." This is extremely significant because the work of God is not a multiplicity of human activities as the religions of men require of those seeking peace with God. *The work of God* is singular—believe, and surrendering to that belief.

This *work of God* levels the "saving" field, giving to all who seek after God, equal access to the salvation He freely offers through His Son, Jesus Christ. God has made *the work* of salvation so simple and achievable that anyone, from any walk of life, can *work* it—that is, *believe in Jesus Christ whom He has sent*, and surrender to that belief.

However, I must hasten to point out that this singular act of believing can lead to a diversity of works which God had already prearranged and pre-packaged in the incorruptible seed of Christ's spirit-life within the believer. All he has to do is simply walk (*not work*) in them as the Holy

Spirit empowers and guides him from within. What do the Scriptures say?

> *For we are His workmanship, created in Christ Jesus for good works, which God prepared beforehand so that we would walk in them.*

Ephesians 2:8-10

Please understand that the very day we received Christ as our personal Savior and Lord, God *created* us anew *in Him*. God had absolutely no interest in fixing or upgrading our sinful, Adam nature. Instead, He started over. GOD CREATED NEW LIFE! We were BORN AGAIN of Him (John 1:12-13)! That's not a theological motive or idea to be debated in the halls of seminaries or Bible colleges! It is the eternal truth of a real life, generated through grace, by the Spirit of God! God started a brand new race, in an eternal, spirit dimension. Our inner spirit-man is a life that was created to win, because it was born again from the incorruptible seed of the Universal First-Class Winner—Jesus Christ.

Believing God, and surrendering to that belief, is our ONLY work in the plan of redemption.

Finding True Rest

Our belief in, and surrender to, this Jesus-life in our spirit, is the only work that God has called us to do in His plan of redemption. We must believe in who Jesus is—the Messiah of God; what He taught; what He did (including Calvary); what He promised; and surrender our thoughts and lives to those beliefs. This Jesus, whom we are called to believe, invites us to take His yoke and learn from Him. Let us read this invitation in Matthew 11:28-30:

> *Come to Me, all who are weary and heavy-laden, and I will give you rest.* [29]*Take My yoke upon you and learn from Me, for I am gentle and humble in heart, and you will find rest for your souls.* [30]*For My yoke is easy, and My burden is light.*

Matthew 11:28-30

In this very simple invitation, Jesus graciously offers all believers the key to a life of victory, peace and rest. However, so many who have often read and even memorized this priceless gem of Christ's promises, have fallen short of its blessing because they have either missed the key to possessing it, or failed at using the key altogether.

Consequently, these precious souls have failed to find Christ's promised rest from the heavy burdens of life.

Take Christ's Yoke:

The inestimable key for the victorious, restful life in Christ Jesus is the believer's acceptance of the Savior's yoke. This acceptance requires, first and foremost, a clear understanding of what that yoke is; and second, an act of abiding faith to embrace and live with it. What is Christ's yoke—for He did say, "take My yoke" in the text? Jesus applied an agricultural term in common usage in His day to describe the relationship He sought with His followers.

By definition, a yoke is a wooden instrument used to join a pair of oxen or other draft animals so they can work together to pull heavy loads. However, Christ's usage of the yoke metaphor does not really refer to any physical bonding. On the contrary, Christ's yoke points to the mystical union of spirits—His Spirit with the spirit of those who choose to join themselves to Him. The Bible states very clearly:

> *But the one who <u>joins</u> himself to the Lord is <u>one spirit</u> with Him.*

1 Corinthians 6:17

The yoke that binds or joins the believer to Christ is Christ's own spirit within the believer. No finite mind can fully explain the extensive, eternal implications of the one-spirit union Christ shares with all those who have received Him as Savior and Lord. Nevertheless, the Savior's invitation to take His yoke is a call for full recognition and acceptance of the oneness of spirit we share with Him and with every other believer. This was the burden of Jesus' prayer before He went to Calvary.

The yoke of Christ is the mystical union of His Spirit with ours.

> *"I do not ask on behalf of these alone, but for those also who believe in Me through their word; [21]that they may all be one; even as You, Father, are in Me and I in You, that they also may be in Us, so that the world may believe that You sent Me. [22]The glory which You have given Me I have given to them, that they may be one, just as We are one; [23]I in them and You in Me, that they may be perfected in unity, so that the world may know that You sent Me, and loved them, even as You have loved Me.*

John 17:20-21

The great theme of this prayer is unmistakable. It's all about oneness, unity, and convincing the world about the authenticity of God's Messiah, Jesus Christ. The "*you in me*," "*I in you*," "*I in them*," and "*they in us*" language is strictly *spirit talk*, or *yoke language*, if you please. This type of intricate, intertwining, invasive union is totally impossible in flesh. It is reserved only for the realm of the spirit. Moreover, the fact that Christ repeated this *spirit talk—yoke language* three times in this one prayer makes it very significant indeed. This mystical, inseparable union of spirits—Spirit to spirits—is the bond of perfection (John 17:23), and the one irrefutable argument that will convince the world that the Jesus of the Bible is real, and that all that He did and claimed are true.

The major reason our world is not yet convinced about the claims of Christianity is because we, Jesus' professed followers, have failed to recognize and accept His yoke. Consequently, we continue to divide His body by our carnal worldview of what His kingdom is all about, and by our human perspectives and definitions of what being a born-again Christian really is. Religious formalism, pious sectarianism and controlling institutionalism have made professed Christianity the most divided religion in the world; and Saturday or Sunday mornings, a confused, fleshly caricature—religious form without authentic power (2 Timothy 3:5)—of what the yoke of Christ really represents.

The goal of Christ's prayer in John 17 is the manifestation of the mystical yoke He share with His followers. In His final petition, He asked the Father to allow the love which they (He and the Father) shared to be deposited in the same measure in His disciples—that is, "*I in them*," (John 17:26). What a way to end a prayer—*I in them*! As if to say, "*Don't forget the yoke, Father*." The love of the Father is in the yoke Christ shares with His disciples—spirit oneness.

Learn from Christ:

In addition to taking His yoke, Christ encouraged all His followers to learn from Him. This means that we all need to pay very close attention to His life and His relationship with His Father while He was here on earth. From a very early age, the Savior *recognized*, *accepted* and *practiced* the identity He shared with His Father in heaven. No doubt, His surrogate parents, Joseph and Mary, rehearsed in His childlike ear the mysteries surrounding His birth, as spoken by the angel Gabriel and effected through the ministry of the Holy Spirit. Little did they realize that by the tender age of 12, their "Son" already had a very clear understanding of His true identity, and already had surrendered Himself completely to His one-Spirit union (or yoke) with His Father. This relationship He cherished and protected above and beyond any other known to Him.

Consequently, Joseph and Mary were caught totally off-guard when, during His first official visit to the temple in Jerusalem, Jesus would meet their self-justifying parental reprimand with His own gentle rebuke: "*Why is it that you were looking for Me? Did you not know that I had to be in My Father's house*" (Luke 2:49)? In the Authorized King James version of the Bible, the second of these two questions is rendered thus: "*wist ye not that I must be about my Father's business?*"

Joseph and Mary had lost track of the Savior because they were preoccupied with their own interests during the temple visit. Not until a day's journey on their way back home, did they suddenly realize that the lad Jesus was not with them. It took them three harrowing days to find the most precious Gift ever given to the care of erring mortals. Where did they find Him? Exactly where the yoke of the Father planted Him—that is, in God's house, doing His Father's business.

However, instead of acknowledging their mistake in taking their earthly eyes off the heavenly Prize, they attempted to justify themselves via their parental authority. However, Jesus' response revealed to them that He recognized and surrendered His allegiance to an authority infinitely higher than their own. Many years later, His earthly family had another rude awakening when they sought to pull

Him away from His Father's business. Jesus was very forthright in telling the family messenger and the crowd gathered about Him that His only true family members were, and are, those who share the Father's yoke with Him (Mark 3:31-35). What an example for all who would believe in Him!

It was the Father's yoke, the one-Spirit union with the Divine Sender, that gave strength and focus to the Savior's true identity, and directed the course of His entire earthly existence. Throughout His earthly sojourn, Christ never lost touch—not even for a moment—with His true identity and union with His heavenly Father. Everything He ever taught and did was the by-product of this heavenly yoke.

Christ union with His Father was the abiding theme and directional focus of His life.

His union with the Father was the abiding theme and directional focus of His life. John, more than any other of the disciples, reflected this in his testimony regarding the Savior's life:

> *"Truly, truly, I say to you, <u>the Son can do nothing of Himself</u>, unless it is something He sees the Father doing; for <u>whatever the Father does</u>, these things <u>the Son also does</u> in <u>like manner</u>."*

John 5:19

"I can do nothing on My own initiative. As I hear, I judge; and My judgment is just, because I do not seek My own will, but the will of Him who sent Me."

John 5:30

"I and the Father are one."

John 10:30

"For I did not speak of my own accord, but the Father who sent me commanded me what to say and how to say it. ⁵⁰I know that his command leads to eternal life. So whatever I say is just what the Father has told me to say."

John 12:49-50, NIV

The Father did the Work:

Notice, in all of the above references that Christ attributed all of His words and work, not to Himself, but to the Father whose yoke He gladly bore. In John 14, the Savior's characterization of this yoke (one-Spirit union with

His Father) seems to find its clearest expression, as Jesus prepared His disciples for His imminent departure from the world. Although the entire chapter is quite revealing, we will concentrate on the Master's response to Philip's inquiry, "*Lord, show us the Father, and it is enough for us*" (John 14:8). Jesus said to him,

> "*Have I been so long time with you, and yet hast thou not known me, Philip? He that hath seen me hath seen the Father; and how sayest thou then, Show us the Father?*"

John 14:9, KJV

The Father declared Himself through Christ's voice— "*Have I been so long with you, and yet you have not come to know Me, Philip?*" Then Christ confirmed the Father's declaration by stating, "*He who has seen Me has seen the Father.*"[1] This was such an awe-inspiring moment—much like Jesus' transfiguration—that I am not even sure if the disciples fully recognized what had transpired. The Father and Christ spoke through one voice to reveal the sublime union and activities of Spirit-life, which He further attempted to explain in the following two verses.

> "*Believest thou not that <u>I am in the Father</u>,*

and <u>the Father in me</u>? The words that I speak unto you <u>I speak not of myself</u>: but <u>the Father that dwelleth in me</u>, HE DOETH THE WORKS. [11]Believe me that <u>I am in the Father</u>, and <u>the Father in me</u>: or else believe me for <u>the very works' sake</u>."

John 14:10-11, KJV

The Spirit-Spirit union between Christ and the Father reflects an indwelling duality which allows the will of the One to be perfectly expressed through the life of the Other. Consequently, Christ told His disciples that the words which He spoke came directly from His Father, and all that He did was really performed by the Father who lived in Him. Notice in verse 11 above, He told Philip and the other disciples that even though they did not fully understand the Father-Son, Spirit-Spirit union, they could believe Him for the very works' sake—truly, the Father's sake, the One who was really doing the works. Christ expressed this very idea to the Jews who questioned His authority and His direct link to God, the Father.

"If I do not do the works of My Father, do not believe Me; [38]but if I do them, though you do not believe Me, <u>believe the works</u>, <u>so that you</u>

> <u>*may know and understand that the Father is*</u>
> <u>*in Me, and I in the Father*</u>."

John 10:37-38

The apostle Paul expressed this empowering Spirit-union truth as God working in (and through) Christ, reconciling the world unto Himself (2 Corinthians 5:19). This was the vital key to the Savior's life of success and victory. The omnipotent, heavenly Father was the unfailing power driving all Christ's works. Consequently, Christ never took the glory

The omnipotent, heavenly Father was the unfailing power driving all Christ's works

to Himself for anything He did, because He knew quite well that it was the Father, residing in Him, that really performed the works. He lived to glorify His Father, and the Father delighted in honoring His Son by working miraculously through Him.

It was in the one-Spirit yoke of His Father that the Savior found complete peace and rest, because He allowed the Father, who resided in Him, to do the work. Even in the face of the cruelest abuse, Christ was able to maintain His restful disposition, because He had resigned the keeping of His soul to the unfailing, watchful care of His Father. This is exactly what the Savior wishes to bring to the life of every disciple He has invited to take His yoke. The Word of God speaks very clearly to this very issue:

> *To this you were called, because Christ suffered for you, <u>leaving you an example, that you should follow in His steps</u>.* [22]*He committed no sin, and no deceit was found in His mouth.* [23]*When they hurled their insults at Him, He did not retaliate; when He suffered, He made no threats. Instead, <u>He entrusted himself to Him who judges justly</u>.*

1 Peter 2:21-23, NIV

Christ believed the Father, and that belief led to His complete surrender to His Father's yoke, and this opened the door for the Father to work freely and unobtrusively in and through Him. The blessed assurance of the Father's presence and work—via the yoke—was the source of the Savior's inner security, peace and sweet rest. We have been called to learn from Him (Matthew 11:28-30) by following His flawless example. This leads us to the next phase of learning to live His life—that is, the matter of *focus*.

Focus

Truth Nugget #4: *Whoever and whatever we focus on we become.*

It is in the flawless example of Jesus' life that the believer finds the keys for living the way He did. Christ's invitation to learn from Him is also a call to focus on, and follow, Him. Just as the Savior focused on, and submitted to, the yoke of His Father, so He bids every believer to relate to Him. He knows that the only way we will ever succeed in living His life is the very way He succeeded in living His Father's life—submission to the Spirit-to-Spirit (or one-Spirit) yoke. Through faith, we too must surrender daily to the Word of God and the spirit-to-Spirit union we share with our Savior and our heavenly Father.

The Bible says that because we share His spirit and His life as His brethren, we shall ultimately be like Him—that is, as He is now—when He shall appear in glory (1 John 3:2). But while we wait, we must be guided, not by what we think, feel or desire, but solely by what Christ thinks, feels and desires. We must remain focused on Him, not on our Adam selves. Here are some words of wisdom:

> *Now <u>the Lord is the Spirit</u>, and <u>where the Spirit of the Lord is, there is liberty</u>. [18]But we*

all, with unveiled face, <u>beholding as in a mirror</u> the glory of the Lord, are <u>being transformed into the same image from glory to glory, just as from the Lord</u>, <u>the Spirit</u>.

Corinthians 3:17-18

Divine transformation is a work of the Spirit of Christ influencing the spirit of the believer (Romans 8:16); not the work of flesh trying to become spiritual. The latter is an exhausting exercise in futility and an affront to God. However, when the believer stays focused on the Christ in him through the Christ he daily encounters in the Word, the mystery of God's will and work begin to unfold in his life. As the beauty and glory of Christ—instead of self—become the *unalterable* image in his mental mirror, he is strangely changed, from glory to glory, into the image of his Lord, by the Holy Spirit.

How easy is living the born-again life, really? It is *Christ-easy* for the believer, as it was *God-easy* for the Savior when He walked among men. We must learn from Him and do as He did. The God in Him did the work. In the same manner, the God and Christ in us will do the work if we surrender our "foolish" will and ways for Christ's yoke. The Savior depended totally upon the life of the Father within Him; so must we depend on His life within us. This life must be our daily focus and attention. What we focus on we ultimately become, for our focus determines our reality.

Now, here is a daily confession and supporting scriptures to help us keep our focus on the reality of our born-again life from heaven:

WHO AM I, REALLY?[3]

I AM A NEW CREATION IN CHRIST; A BORN-AGAIN SPIRIT BEING; BORN OF INCORRUPTIBLE SEED BY THE WORD, AND THROUGH THE POWER OF THE HOLY SPIRIT WHO OPERATES IN ME. I LIVE IN MY SAVIOR, AND MY SAVIOR LIVES IN ME. THE FATHER ALSO LIVES IN JESUS; WE ARE A PERFECT UNITY. I AM MOST CERTAINLY A KINGDOM CITIZEN, WHOSE LIFE IS FROM ABOVE AND NOT FROM BELOW. I AM INVINCIBLE, UNSTOPPABLE, AND IMMOVABLE, BECAUSE I WALK IN THE AUTHORITY OF MY EXALTED SAVIOR. I SUFFER NO LACK; I HAVE EVERYTHING I NEED; FOR ALL THINGS BELONG TO ME SINCE MY LORD AND I ARE ONE. I AM MY FATHER'S *SUPREME MAKEOVER—THE SPIRITUAL EDITION*.

SCRIPTURES: 2 Corinthians 5:17; 1 Peter 1:23; John 1:12, 13; 3:6; 1 Corinthians 6:17; John 14:20; 17:21-23; Philippians 3:20; Ephesians 1:15-23; Philippians 4:19; 1 Corinthians 3:21-23

Truth Nuggets Summary

1. *If I do not recognize, understand and live by my true identity in Christ, I can never gain dominion over satan and sin.*

2. *The born-again person must accept his union with Christ and his heavenly origin as the realities through which he views and interacts with the world.*

3. *Who and what we believe will direct the course of our life.*

4. *Whoever and whatever we focus on, we become.*

Notes:

1. See Ruthven J. Roy, *Imitating God,* (Berrien Springs, MI: Rehoboth Publishing, 2010), pp 92-94, for a full explanation of Jesus' response to Philip's request.

2. See also Hebrews 8:8-12 for the amplification of that same covenant promise. Pay very close attention to the work that God has promised to do and to the amazing transforming result. Everyone who believes will know the Lord intuitively and experientially.

3. Ruthven J. Roy, *Imitating God*, p. 96.

For in Him all the fullness of Deity dwells in bodily form, [10]and in Him you have been made complete . . .

Colossians 2:9-10

Chapter 7

BORN AGAIN:
THE FULLNESS

As we take a closer look at Christ's conversation with Philip and the other disciples in John 14, we pick up on a very incredible statement by the Master in verse 12. He said, *"Verily, verily, I say unto you, He that believeth on me, the works that I do shall he do also; and greater works than these shall he do; because I go unto my Father."* However, it is best to read this verse in connection with the two previous verses to get the real substance of Christ's message.

> *"Believest thou not that I am in the Father, and the Father in me? The words that I speak unto you I speak not of myself: but the Father that dwelleth in me, he doeth the works. [11] Believe me that I am in the Father, and the Father in me: or else believe me for the very works' sake. [12] Verily, verily, I say unto you, He that believeth on me, the works that I do shall he do also; and greater works than these shall he do; because I go unto my Father."*

> John 14:10-12, KJV

Truth Nugget #1: *Works greater than Christ's are possible for me only after I come to truly believe and surrender to the reality of the spirit-oneness I share with God, through Jesus Christ.*

The very first thing that we must observe is that the common denominator of these three verses, as well as for doing the greater works Christ spoke about, is the disciples' belief in Him. Notice the question, "*Do you believe . . .?*" (verse10); then the plea, "*Believe Me*" (twice in verse 11); and finally, the declaration, "*He that believes Me . . .*" (verse 12). The Bible reminds us that *without faith it is impossible to please him: for he that cometh to God must believe that he is, and that he is a rewarder of them that diligently seek him* (Hebrews 11:6). Jesus also said that "'*if you can?' All things are possible to him who believes*" (Mark 9:23).

Now, if we can believe, Jesus said that we will be able to perform works just like Him, and even greater than Him, because He went to the Father on our behalf. Why did He go to the Father? So the Spirit of the Father and the Son (one Spirit of Truth) could take up residence in us—*to do the works!*

> "*I will ask the Father, and He will give you another Helper, that He may be with you forever; ¹⁷that is the Spirit of truth, whom the*

world cannot receive, because it does not see
Him or know Him, but you know Him because
He abides with you and will be <u>in you</u>. ¹⁸I will
not leave you as orphans; <u>I will come to you</u>."

John 14:16-18

The Holy Spirit is the unerring witness of the presence of both the Father and the Son within every believer. He is the divine guarantee that God will finish the work He started in us, through Jesus Christ. Although He was about to go to the Father, Jesus told His disciples that He would come to them. How was this ever going to be possible? The Holy Spirit, whom Jesus was going to send from the Father, was going to be the living reality of His presence among and in His disciples. He is also the One who confirms in our spirit that we are indeed God's children (Romans 8:16). Consequently, the Holy Spirit is the divine expression of both the Father and our Lord, Jesus Christ. Jesus attempted to explain this mysterious reality to His disciples in a concise, mind-boggling statement two verses later:

> *The Holy Spirit is the unerring witness of the presence of both the Father and the Son within every believer.*

At that day ye shall know that <u>I am in my</u>

Father, and ye in me, and I in you.

John 14:20, KJV

"That day" refers to the day that the inexplicable witness of the Holy Spirit illumines the spirit and mind of the believer regarding his true identity and position in Jesus Christ. When "that day" happens for the believer, he would suddenly realize that Christ is in the Father (one Spirit—John 10:30); he (the believer) is in Christ (one spirit—1 Corinthians 6:17), who Himself (Christ), is in the Father. Moreover, that Christ who is in the Father, is also in the believer, uniting the Father with him (the believer). Jesus made this very plain in John 14:23, when He confirmed:

> "... *If a man loves me, he will keep my words: and my Father will love him, and we will come unto him, and make our abode with him.*"

John 14:23, KJV

God and Christ living permanently within the believer's spirit through the witness of the Holy Spirit, is the goal and essence of the born-again experience. This is *Divine Fullness*. The author encourages all the readers of this book to take a full week, or as much time as possible to meditate upon the incalculable implications of this glorious truth. Believing and living the presence of *Divine Fullness* is the immovable platform from which the believer is able to do the greater works of which Christ spoke, because God and Christ—through the Holy Spirit—are at work in him.

Sadly, unbelieving "believers" fail to recognize, accept and practice their true identity in Christ. Therefore, they miss the benefits of their spirit-to-Spirit union with the Savior, the Father, and with one another. As a result, instead of experiencing the power of the unified Spirit of Christ among all believers, the ruling spirit of fallen Adam continues to define their existence, relationships and total spiritual experience.

God and Christ living permanently within the believer's spirit is the goal and essence of the born-again experience.

However, whenever "that day" occurs for those of us who truly believe, we will suddenly discover—as did the disciples at, and after, Pentecost—that we are never alone. We will know the truth that God, the Father, and the Lord, Jesus Christ, are not far away in the distant heavens, but are one with us through the personal, intuitive witness of the Holy Spirit. We will know that the divine Presence, though unseen, is very active in our every situation, constantly working for our good (Romans 8:28). When that epiphany arrives, then we will believe and know by experience that *it is God who is at work in us [you]*, *both to will* and *to work for His good pleasure* (Philippians 2:13).

Divine Causation

Truth Nugget #2: *I am not the producer of my successes and victories in my Christian walk. God is.*

This matter of God's dwelling and operating within the spirit of the born-again believer is the fulfillment of God's covenant promise to His believing children. He said:

> "*Moreover, I will give you a new heart and put a new spirit within you; and I will remove the heart of stone from your flesh and give you a heart of flesh. [27]I will put My Spirit within you and cause you to walk in My statutes, and you will be careful to observe My ordinances.*"

Ezekiel 36:26-27

The most phenomenal thing about this covenant is that God is doing ALL the work. He will give us a new heart—a compliant moral center. He will give us a new spirit—pointing to spirit regeneration or the born-again experience. He will put His Spirit within our spirit—establishing Spirit-spirit union. Most important and significant is the fact that God will *cause* us to walk in obedience to ALL His decrees and laws. ALL that is left for us to do is to BELIEVE that God will do what He said He would (and has done), and to SURRENDER to that belief. We must give up on the "I" in us (our self-will or flesh-life), and replace it by the "Christ" in us (our Christ-will or spirit-life).

Divine causation is the direct outworking of the power of God's life, initiating, sustaining and empowering the life of the believer. It represents the continuous stream of divine virtue flowing in spirit-life that was born of the Spirit, God. This phenomenon of heavenly grace does not harbor a single thread of fallen humanity. As a matter of fact, it is this embedded, incorruptible quality which makes born-again spirit-life invincible against sin and disobedience; and which *causes* it to operate ONLY in righteousness and truth.

The Spirit used a rather natural event to illustrate this powerful truth me. Early one morning, after a freak storm had rolled through our neighborhood during the night, I saw a young bird jumping around on our front lawn, attempting to flee from my presence. I soon realized that the little creature and

> *Divine causation is the direct outworking of the power of God's life, initiating, sustaining and empowering the life of the believer.*

its nest had been blown from their safe haven in the tree which stood in the middle of lawn area. I also observed that the bird's distressed mother was not very far away keeping a watchful eye over her hapless offspring.

I drew my wife's attention to the plight of the young bird, which, by then, had taken shelter under one of our garden plants. Around mid-morning, my wife called out to me because she had just witness the bird's mother deposit a worm into the open throat of the youngster. I immediately came to the scene again, and we both sat around waiting for the mother to return. Sure enough, she lighted from a nearby tree, unto the grass, with a worm dangling from her beak. Then she hopped over to her vulnerable young, and fed her again.

My wife was so amazed and tickled at the sight that she unconsciously turned to me and said, "Wow, how does she do that?" Just when I was about to say, "because of instinct"—the explanation I learned in middle-school science class—the phrase, *Divine causation*, just pop into my spirit. At that very moment, I heard those words rolling off my tongue, as God began to open up to me the revelation of something much bigger in the spirit realm than the natural realm of "the birds and the bees."

Here is the revelation on the fallen bird and its hovering mother. Resident in every created thing is the unerring divine principle of embedded functionality which *causes* every creature not only to produce after its kind (Genesis 1:11-12, 21, 24-25), but also to function naturally in either unique or sometime similar ways. The mother bird did not need any external rule of conduct, or any form of coercion to make her watch over, or feed, her young. This behavior was already built into her by her Creator before she was even hatched from her egg.

In the very same manner, when a person is born-again of the Spirit, he does not need external system of rules to govern his behavior. *Divine causation* is already at work in the incorruptible seed of his born-again spirit, directing him to walk naturally (really spiritually) in the will of the God. His obedience, therefore, is not the work of his flesh—the "I" in him trying to please God; but the work of his spirit— the Christ in his inner spirit-man, giving him both the desire and power to obey. This is the very "heart and soul" of salvation and the unfailing engine that drives the born-again experience.

Consequently, it is very important for all born-again believers to keep in remembrance that it is the Christ in us (Galatians 2:20), who daily empowers us to love and obey Him. The same principle held true for Christ. It was God in Him (the Savior), who was reconciling the world unto Himself (2 Corinthians 5:19). Understanding, accepting and practicing this truth is the **key** to living the born-again life successfully. Jesus puts it simply in this way:

173

"I am the vine, you are the branches; he who abides in Me and I in him, he bears much fruit, for apart from Me you can do nothing."

John 15:5

Abiding in the Vine is the Master's call for us to keep our focus on Him and His life in our spirit. This is another way of Jesus saying to us, "Take My yoke upon you and learn from Me" (Matthew 11:29). The perfect union of Christ's Spirit with ours (1 Corinthians 6:17) is our only hope for living the way our Savior did. Apart from this union, we can do absolutely nothing to truly please God.

The perfect union of Christ's Spirit with ours is our only hope for living the way our Savior did.

Our inner spirit-man is a spirit of submission and cooperation which always walks in harmony with heaven. He was created that way and can do no less, because he is the incorruptible spirit-seed of Christ (Ephesians 2:10; 2 Peter 1:3-4). He is always Christ-driven. Our flesh, on the other hand, is a spirit of opposition and disobedience, operating under the deceptive power of the prince of darkness (Ephesians 2:1-3). Really, it represents anything and everything we do by thought, word, or action that is "me-driven" or self-directed.

Interestingly, the Holy Spirit gave me the revelation

one day that the word FLESH, when turned backwards gives HSELF—Hidden Self. That's exactly what flesh is, deceptive self that is always waiting for expression in some way, shape or form. Is it any wonder that Jesus says that the very first step in following Him is self-denial? Hidden Self (or FLESH) is what stands in the way of everything God wants to do for us, in us, and through us, always seeking to exalt its wisdom above the revealed will of God.

Moreover, the more empowered self becomes, the more resistant self is to surrender to God's demands. So many of God's children are being deceived into thinking they can give better service to God through self-improvement. Although God has given them the perfect, incorruptible seed-life of Jesus in their spirit which requires absolutely no improvement, they spend their days on earth struggling to improve what God has already consigned for destruction. If God could have done some improvement on Adam to make him right before Him, He would not have required ALL Adam's descendants to be born again of the Spirit in order to be saved.

Quit Working on "Old Junk"!

Truth Nugget #3: *No matter how hard I work on my Adam self I will never be able to bring it to perfection through obedience.*

God has given ALL a successful way out of our failing humanity—i.e. He created a new life for ALL in Christ Jesus (Ephesians 2:10). Our trouble is that we have become so used to our life in the flesh that we fail to embrace our life in the spirit. If we are to succeed in living our Christ-life, we must change our focus and our practice. We must quit working on "old junk". The apostle Paul says

> "that, in reference to your former manner of life, you *lay aside* *the old self*, which is being corrupted in accordance with the lusts of deceit, [23]and that you *be renewed* in *the spirit of your mind*, [24]and *put on* the *new self*, which *in the likeness of God* has been created in *righteousness* and *holiness of the truth*.

> Ephesians 4:22-24

Identity practice is all about learning how to walk in one's spirit life, while refusing to support all the self-centered or fleshly activities of one's natural life. The Bible states very clearly that if we walk by the Spirit's influence we will not fulfill the desires of our flesh (Galatians 5:16). It would be totally misleading for one to think that this counsel was for the natural Adam man. It is absolutely impossible for flesh to walk by the Spirit. Although the self-made or self-improved man—really carnal before God—may perform religious works, it does not make him or the works he does spiritual. He just cannot walk by the Spirit.

Only one born of the Spirit is capable of walking by the Spirit. It takes spirit to walk by the Spirit! This is who the born-again inner spirit-man is, but he lives in a fleshly tent called the human self. Therefore, the counsel is relevant to him. In other words, Paul is saying, "do not allow your tent to rule you." In the scripture that heads this section, the apostle says that in reference to our former life, we must put off the old self (Ephesians 4:22).

Simply speaking, this admonition means ***stop being*** (assuming only the natural existence or the "I am only human" mentality); ***stop thinking*** (leaning on self and human reason); and ***stop living*** (behaving or walking through life) like fallen descendants of Adam. Stop focusing on the rightness or wrongness of your outer-man. Fleshly assessment is worthless, for

Only one born of the Spirit is capable of walking by the Spirit. It takes spirit to walk by the Spirit!

Adam can never be right before God regardless of his noblest actions or moral aspirations. The Bible says that this Adam person we behold in the mirror is corrupt after (or controlled by) his/her deceitful lusts (Ephesians 4:22).

Rather than being fixated on our Adam self, Paul says that we ought to put on, and keep on, our new self. In other words, we should *start being* (practicing our divine spirit existence); *start trusting* (depending on God and faith, instead of self and reason); and *start imitating* (living like) our Father in heaven, through the example Christ, our elder Brother—Ephesians 5:1-2; Matthew 11:29; 16:24.

Successful, born-again living is truly a matter of focus. Who is getting my daily attention? Is it the old man of "self" or the new man of Christ; the outer man of my flesh or the inner man of my spirit? The believer must choose daily to live out of the reality of his inner spirit-man, giving preference to his needs and desires over those of his natural self-life. As a rule of thumb, spirit must be nurtured and fed before pursuing any course of action that pertains to the support of the "self." This, in essence, is what Jesus meant when He said: *"If anyone wishes to come after Me, he must deny himself, and take up his cross <u>daily</u> and follow Me"* (Luke 9:223).

Ultimately, born-again spirit living is the daily spiritual discipline of connecting with, and engaging, one's true identity in Christ, while at the same time keeping flesh (hidden self or the "I" in me) crucified through denial and starvation. Paul's counsel to the believers in Rome amplifies this practice in one powerful sentence: *". . . put on the Lord Jesus Christ, and <u>make no provision</u> for the flesh, to gratify its desires* (Romans 13:14, NRSV).

Making provision or room for the flesh is the same as

giving place to the devil (Ephesians 4:27), for he is the father of flesh. We must stay focused on the Christ in us, so as to deny this stalking, roaring lion (1 Peter 5:8) the opportunity he seeks to rule and devour our lives through his ceaseless enticements. In this regard, we must guard our senses from the countless distractions he hurls at us from the limitless flashpoints he has established in the world.

ONLY One Life to Live — JESUS'

> *For you have died and your life is hidden with Christ in God. ⁴When Christ, **who is our life**, is revealed, then you also will be revealed with Him in glory.*

Colossians 3:3-4

From God's view of reality, the former life of His born-again children is dead, buried and totally inconsequential in all matters pertaining to their eternal salvation. God's priority and focus is the life of His Son in every believer, not the lingering distractions of satan manifesting in their flesh. Our Father's desire is for our faith to lay hold of His reality so that we can

God's priority and focus is the life of His Son in every believer, not the lingering distractions of satan manifesting in their flesh.

179

share His focus. God wants us to believe Him for who He is: A God who cannot lie. He wants us to believe Him for what He completed in Christ and for all that He said in His Word. Without such faith, we cannot please Him (Hebrews 11:6), and, therefore, cannot fully benefit from all that He offers.

Believe God! Christ is now our life—not the person in the mirror. He/she can only reflect the presence and power of Christ's life within us. Whenever we begin to believe and live this truth, we will begin to experience the power of its reality.

The Fullness

Truth Nugget #4: *The intrinsic goal of born-again life is to experience the fullness of God through the love of Jesus Christ.*

> *For this reason I bow my knees before the Father, [15]from whom every family in heaven and on earth derives its name, [16]that He would grant you, according to the riches of His glory, to be <u>strengthened with power</u> <u>through His Spirit</u> in <u>**the inner man**</u>, [17]so that <u>Christ</u> may <u>dwell in your hearts through faith</u>; and that you, <u>being rooted and grounded in love</u>, [18]may be able to comprehend with all the*

saints what is the breadth and length and height and depth, [19]and <u>to know the love of Christ</u> which surpasses knowledge, that you may be filled up to <u>all the fullness of God</u>.

Ephesians 3:14-19

The work of the Holy Spirit is always directed to the inner man of the believer's spirit; never the outer man of natural human intelligence. The strength and power to live the born-again life successfully always come from within the spirit of the child of God, because that's where Christ and the Father dwell through the witness of the Spirit (John 14:23; Romans 8:16). This life is rooted in love because it sprung forth from the God Who is Love (John 1:12-13; 1 John 4:8).

The clause, *"being rooted and grounded in love,"* in the above text, is connected to the *"you"* that comes before it. When taken together, they point to a strong sense of divine existence, identity and belonging that must never be confused with anything that is of earth or Adam. The life of the believer has a completely new root—LOVE—that is constantly nourished by the Holy Spirit (Romans 5:5), as the life it supports grows into the fullness of God—Jesus Christ. The Word of God says that *in Him all the fullness of Deity dwells in bodily form, [10]and in Him you have been made complete .* . . (Colossians 2:9-10). Yes! Born-again life is a tree of love that grows up into full measure and stature of the life of Jesus Christ in every possible way (Ephesians 4:13-15).

How can I tell that I have been born again?

How can one tell that he/she has been born again of the incorruptible seed of God? There is only one answer to that question, and that is, when one's life and attitude are characterized by the abiding fruit of love. Jesus said, "*By this shall ALL men know that you are my disciples if you have LOVE one for another*" (John 13:35). The Scriptures also say, "*You will know them by their fruits*" (Matthew 7:16, 20); and that *the fruit of the Spirit is LOVE...* (Galatians 5:22); and *if anyone does not have the Spirit of Christ, he does not belong to Him* (Romans 8:9).

It is the root that bear the fruit; not the fruit the root. One can tell what type of fruit a tree will produce by simply identifying its root. "Just show me your root and I'll tell you your fruit, long before there is any on your tree." The born-again believer does not need to concentrate his energy and effort on bearing the fruit of love in his life. He already has the root within his spirit for the production of that fruit. All he has to do is to nurture and water it with the abundant Word and Spirit of Love.

Let the knowledge of Christ love—that He has for you—daily fill your thoughts, consume your energies and guide your experience in Him. When this love becomes your own, it will supersede your love for everything else, and will manifest itself in loving, compassionate service to a world that's hungering for it. That is when you will know, by experience, the love of Christ, and be filled with the fullness of born-again Life—God's.

Look at yourself every day in the mirror and confess aloud three times—seven times for divine completeness: "I AM THE RIGHTEOUSNESS OF GOD IN JESUS CHRIST. I HAVE DIVINE FULLNESS IN ME! Now, believe it! Go out in the strength of Lord within, and live it!

Truth Nuggets Summary

1. *Works greater than Christ's are possible for me only after I come to truly believe and surrender to the reality of the spirit-oneness I share with God, through Jesus Christ.*
2. *I am not the producer of my successes and victories in my Christian walk: God is.*
3. *No matter how hard I work on our Adam self I will never be able to bring him to perfection through obedience.*
4. *The intrinsic goal of born-again life is to experience the fullness of God through the love of Jesus Christ.*

Conclusion

Through this volume we have discovered that the born-again life has absolutely nothing to do with the former life of Adam, because God created a completely new spiritual existence in Jesus Christ for everyone who believe and receive Him as his personal Savior. Most people do not connect with this new life because it is not visible to the naked eye and operates in a reality completely independent and altogether different from the one with which they are so familiar. Nevertheless, it is real and amazingly powerful, very much like the invisible wind, whose path cannot be harnessed or directed, but whose potent presence can be felt, seen and heard (John 3:8).

Additionally, we have seen that the Bible states very clearly that whatsoever is born of the Spirit—and God is Spirit—is *spirit*, not just *spiritual* (John 3:6); and that there is a clear difference between the two terms. As we have noted, *spirit* points to what a person or thing is, whereas *spiritual* indicates how a person or thing acts or behaves. It is totally impossible for that which is carnal to become spirit or act spiritual. Consequently, the born-again life is not that of the Adam man attempting to become spiritual by the performance of religious acts. To the contrary, it is the inner spirit-man of the believer, operating through his Adamic host, the pre-ordained works of God deposited in him at his creation. Remember the inspired declaration:

> *For we are His workmanship, <u>created</u> in*
> *Christ Jesus <u>for good works</u>, which God*
> *<u>prepared beforehand</u> so that we would walk*
> *in them.*

Ephesians 2:10

> *"Moreover, <u>I will</u> give you a new heart and put*
> *a new spirit within you; and <u>I will</u> remove the*
> *heart of stone from your flesh and give you a*
> *heart of flesh. [27]<u>I will</u> put My Spirit within you*
> *and <u>**cause**</u> <u>you to walk</u> in My statutes, and you*
> *will be careful to observe My ordinances."*

Ezekiel 36:26-27

As was stated earlier, both these scriptures brings into very clear view the truth that God is the One who created us anew *in Christ*—not in Adam—for the good works, which He, Himself, prepared beforehand for us to simply manifest in our daily walk. In Ezekiel, God is also the One who is doing the *"causing"* of obedience—not man trying desperately to make it happen. Most certainly, then, salvation is totally the work of God and the complete surrender of man to that work. It is our faith in God that leads to this surrender, so that the Almighty can work in us *both to will and to do of His good pleasure* (Philippians 2:13).

However, in order for the child of God to work (really surrender) cooperative, harmoniously and effectively with the presence of God within Him, it is important for him to have a very clear understanding of, and connection with, his inner spirit-man. In other words, he must recognize, accept and practice the reality of the "Christ" in him, giving Him priority over the "I" or "Me" in him. He has to be renewed in the way his mind operates so that he may be able to walk by his spirit instead of by his flesh (hidden self). To facilitate this transition and transformation, the born-again believer must discipline his mind and soul to walk only by the Word of God.

Just as Christ lived by every word of the Father, so must all those who choose to follow Him. The Word reveals the very thoughts of the Almighty, expressed in human language. It is Spirit and life, just like the One who breathed Its contents to Its holy writers. Therefore, we must train ourselves to know the Word, trust the Word, and bring the Word to bear upon every thought and decision pertaining to our lives. Moreover, we must re-train our senses to filter everything they receive through the unerring principles and demands of the Word of God.

Regarding this matter, we must ask ourselves these

very tough, thought-provoking questions, and be ready to give the most honest answers: Do I believe what I see or only what the Word says about what I see? Do I believe what I hear or only what the Word says about what I hear? Do I believe what I feel or only what the Word says about what I feel? Do I believe what I, or even others, think or only what the Word says about those thoughts? The answers to these questions are what essentially differentiate the inner spirit-man from the natural life of the believer.

By default, born-again life was pre-designed by God to walk in obedience to every word of God. The resistance to the Word does not come from the inner man of the believer's spirit, but always from the outer man of his flesh which is governed totally by human reason. However, the Spirit and the Word of God are the only realities fitted to direct the incorruptible seed of the believer's inner spirit-life; for they are the Ones which gave birth to that life (1 Peter 1:23).

What Does It Look Like?
How can I tell?

Born-again: What does it really look like? The answer to this question is the same as what Christ gave to Philip when He asked the Savior to show the Father to him and his fellow disciples. Essentially, what Philip asked was: "What does the Father really look like?" Remember Jesus' answer? Here it is again: ". . . *He who has seen Me has seen the Father* . . ." John 14:9. So what does born-again really look like? It looks like the Christ, whose incorruptible seed gave birth to it. Born-again life is the living expression of Jesus, the embodiment of what He did and taught, the revelation of the image of the One who created it (Colossians 3:10-11).

Ultimately, all born-again children will be an imitation of their Father—God. This was His purpose for His Son and all His (Jesus) born-again siblings (Hebrews 2:10-15)—to be a reflection of His (God's) love. His Word says that we must imitate Him, and walk in love and light as His dear children (Ephesians 5:1-2, 8; James 1:17). God was the One who determined beforehand that ALL whom He foreknew, would be conformed into the image of His Son, so that Jesus would be the firstborn among many brethren (Romans 8:29).

Therefore, it is most true to say that born-again life is a life of light and love. It is the mirror image of the life of Jesus in the lives of His followers. This is how the world can tell, and we can tell, that we have been born again—by whether or not we are reflecting God's love in our daily lifestyle. "*By this shall all men know that you are my disciples [born-again followers], if you have love one for another*" (John 13:35, bracket mine). I believe the disciples in Antioch represented this perfectly, and, hence, were nicknamed

"Christians"—really, Christ' followers or Christ' shadow (Acts 11:26).

What does your born-again life look like? Does it match up with the character of the Father and the Word that gave birth to it? If not, why not? Maybe it is time for you to change the image in your mental mirror, and allow the "Christ" in you to replace the "I" in your focus. Remember, whatever or whoever you focus on, you will become. If your vision remains stuck on the "I" in you, then you can expect more of the same. However, if you believe God, that Christ is the reality of your life (Colossians 3:4; Galatians 2:20), and if you stay focused on Him instead of yourself, then the mystery of unfolding, divine transformation will begin to appear (2 Corinthians 3:18).

The reality of Christ's anointed presence within you will pervade your thoughts and shape the course of your life. The key element is for you to keep thinking and acting as Christ (not self), surrendering every moment of every day to all the revelations of the Spirit and the Word. Christ's promise to you is that His anointing (through the Holy Spirit) will teach you everything you need to know about Him and the truth He represents. Trust Him. He will finish what He started in you (Philippians 1:6). Remember His words:

But the Counselor, the Holy Spirit, whom the

Father will send in My name, will teach you all things and will remind you of everything I have said to you.

John 14:26, NIV

But when he, the Spirit of truth, comes, <u>he will guide you into all truth</u>. He will not speak on his own; he will speak only what he hears, and <u>he will tell you what is yet to come</u>. [14]He will bring glory to me by taking from what is mine and making it known to you. [15]<u>All that belongs to the Father is mine</u>. That is why I said <u>the Spirit will</u> take from what is mine and <u>make it known to you</u>.

John 16:13-15, NIV

As for you, the anointing you received from Him <u>remains in you</u>, and you do not need anyone to teach you. But as <u>His anointing teaches you</u> about <u>all things</u> and as <u>that anointing is real</u>, not counterfeit—just as it has taught you, <u>remain in Him</u>.

1 John 2:27, NIV

SO LET GOD'S MYSTERY—Christ in you, the hope of glory (Colossians 1:27)—UNFOLD! <u>REMAIN IN HIM</u>, for YOU HAVE BEEN BORN AGAIN INCORRUPTIBLE!

More Exciting Titles
by Dr. Ruthven J. Roy

The Samson Xfile

The Samson Xfile is the intriguing review of the most misunderstood faith-hero in the Bible—Samson. Christian tradition has perpetuated a negative view of this God-warrior; but the mysterious Xfile (Judges 14:4) of God's providence paints an amazingly very different picture. See your life reflected in God's dealing with Samson.

ISBN: 978-0-9717853-1-1 (Hardcover)
978-0-9717853-2-8 (Paperback)

The Explosive Power of Network Discipling

"Every Christian is called to be a disciple of Jesus; and every disciple is called to be a fisher, not just a member!" In this volume Dr. Roy clearly explains Christ's master plan for growing His kingdom. Christ calls everyone to discipleship, not membership.

ISBN: 978-0-9717853-4-2

Imitating God

Imitating God is not only possible, but it is also guaranteed. This book will make available to you the key to your true identity, and will show you, in very simple steps, how to unleash the power of God's life from within you. Get ready to enter into the **God-zone.**

ISBN: 978-0-9717853-3-5

Study Guide: Imitating God

Do not forget this companion Study Guide to go along with this magnificent text. It would greatly enhance your understanding of all the vital issues that pertain to your spiritual identity and living victoriously. Moreover, this Study Guide will provide you with an exciting, hands-on way to share this good news with others.

ISBN: 978-0-9717853-6-6

Unshakeable Kingdom

In the church, yet outside of God's kingdom! What a tragedy! Learn how to avoid the "Nicodemus Syndrome," the common sickness of modern Christianity! Understand true kingdom fitness and why religion is simply not enough. *The kingdom of heaven is NOW; not later! Later is TOO late!* This volume will change your focus and your life in a way that only a miracle from God can. *Seize the moment, and make the decision to enter God's Unshakeable Kingdom now!*

ISBN: 978-0-9717853-3-5

Position Yourself for Success

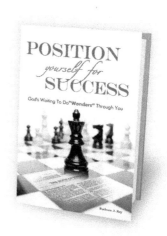

God knew and wrote our success story long before our arrival on this planet. True success depends on how we position ourselves in relation to God's purpose for our existence in this world. This book will help you to discover and pursue it!

ISBN: 978-0-9717853-8-0

Available online or at your local Christian bookstore

For more information, visit www.rjrbooks.com, or write to:
Rehoboth Publishing, P.O. Box 33, Berrien Springs, MI 49103

Contact Information

Dr. Ruthven J. Roy

NETWORK DISCIPLING MINISTRIES
P.O. Box 33
Berrien Springs, MI 49103

Tel: (301) 514-2383
Email: ruthvenroy@gmail.com
Website: www.networkdiscipling.org

RUTHVEN ROY is a discipleship consultant and founder of Network Discipling Ministries. He and his wife Lyris live in Michigan, and are the parents of three precious daughters—Charisa, Lyrisa and Mirisa

CPSIA information can be obtained
at www.ICGtesting.com
Printed in the USA
FFHW01n2208310718
47598247-51108FF